Words and the WORD

Words
and the WORD

KENNETH HAMILTON

WILLIAM B. EERDMANS PUBLISHING COMPANY
Grand Rapids, Michigan

Printed in the United States of America

Bible-Criticism, interpretation
Language and languages- Religious aspects
Myth

Preface

What follows is a slightly expanded version of the Payton Lectures delivered at Fuller Theological Seminary during the Spring Quarter of 1970. The type of ongoing argument which the lecture form demands did not allow much scope for considering the wide variety of viewpoints to be found in contemporary writing on the subject of religious language. By adding a number of footnotes I hope that I have done something — if all too little — to make good this lack. Here I have had opportunity also to mention a few books published since the date when the lectures were prepared, works which would have been featured more prominently had I known of them earlier.

It is a pleasure to record my indebtedness to the faculty, staff, and students at Fuller. The warmth of the welcome I received within the Seminary family made my stay there an unforgettable one. I owe a particular debt to President David A. Hubbard and to Dean Daniel P. Fuller for many personal kindnesses.

Many friends have helped me with this work, both directly and indirectly, too, through discussion and comment. Dr. Paul K. Jewett, Professor of Systematic Theology at Fuller, read the entire manuscript and suggested areas where ambiguities lurked or where further clarification was needed. I am grateful for his comments, even though the text as it stands now may leave some of his queries unanswered — particularly, I fear, the more basic ones. And my thanks go to Miss Lorena Reimer, who typed the manuscript.

KENNETH HAMILTON

The University of Winnipeg

Contents

*

Language and Theology

ONE OF THE UNPRECEDENTED DEVELOPMENTS IN the world of thought in our day is the concentration of interest on the phenomenon of language. Though they agree on hardly anything else, the two great contrasting streams of modern philosophy — the empirical and the existential — agree that the investigation of language is central to the contemporary philosophic quest. As a result, theologians concerned to maintain dialogue with philosophy are also beaming in on the problem of language. Already it is becoming almost impossible for mortal man to keep pace with the volume of theological literature on the subject that now is pouring out of the presses.

To add a few drops to this raging flood may seem a superfluous act; and to think to add anything of consequence to the complex and often abstrusely technical debate concerning the theological implications of theories of language may suggest megalomania. Yet, however formidable this subject appears to be, once it has presented itself it can hardly be avoided.

No one who is committed to the gospel of Jesus Christ can ignore the question of language. Throughout the centuries that gospel has been communicated by preaching, and preaching is the utterance of words. Moreover, preaching Christ is preaching the Word made flesh. Receiving Christ through faith is receiving the living Word of the Father, the God who spoke by the prophets of Israel and who spoke in the beginning to bring all things into being.

9

Yet the divine Word is mediated through human words uttered by the preacher (Rom. 10:14).

The language of preaching is based upon the words of Holy Scripture. But even though the preacher may seek constantly to keep his speech "biblical," he cannot merely repeat scriptural words and phrases. He must follow the common ways of speaking current in his age and locale; and, in order to make his utterance consistent and understandable (to himself and to others), he is compelled to draw upon the language of theology. Theology itself, while equally concerned over keeping to a scriptural basis, must even more deliberately than preaching use language not to be found in the Bible but drawn from culture at large and reflecting the thought-forms available in a particular period of history. Theology, indeed, may be described from the perspective of language as the translation of the gospel into words permitting men to hear God's Word in the context of their cultural situation, and so to reflect upon the truth of the gospel in words that are meaningful to them. Thus it happens that theology is always peculiarly dependent upon the language-forms of the day. It is never exclusively "contemporary," of course, because all language is the product of traditional usage and maintains a living relationship with the past. Yet neither can theological language ever be frozen at any one particular historical moment. It must always take up the task of restating its propositions, even when its purpose is to preserve a particular historical formulation of scriptural truth. This is why theology is an ongoing, never-finished labor in the service of the gospel. Human words change along with the changing face of human culture. The theologian endeavors to state the gospel in words appropriate to his time, and so to interpret previous statements that have served the Christian church in past times that their meaning is not lost because of alterations in language.

My subject, then, is *words and the Word*. It is to ask how the eternal Word is to be heard in the temporal words of men. The question most frequently debated at the moment is how far religious language — or "God-talk" as this is frequently called — can be justified. The specific question of how Scripture and Christian theology stand in relation to the language they use is then regarded as an extension of the universal philosophical question of what language is. But to take this approach, I am convinced, is to misconceive the issue with which the Christian believer and the Christian theologian are properly concerned.

The basic question for the Christian to ask, as I see it, is not how people standing outside the community of faith may be persuaded to admit that the language of faith exhibits a justifiable way of using language. The question is rather one that the believer must put to himself concerning the way in which he makes use of language. It is therefore a theological question, since asking it involves reflection upon the words by means of which faith is communicated and the life of faith explained. The theologian cannot simply accept a rationale of language from a perspective other than his own and then proceed to apply that to his particular concern. He will not avoid the issue of the rationality of theology, or the issue of how theology as a rational discipline is related to other rational disciplines. But neither will be plead for theological discourse to be recognized on any other grounds than that of its claim to be a science of the divine Word.

The theologian is not asking for any special privilege in demanding the right to be considered seriously as a practitioner of a special science, one that operates on a special level and is not to be reduced to the categories of another science. He merely seeks the freedom belonging to every branch of human endeavor. He cannot assume, of course, that theology will be received on its own terms and at its own self-estimate. If he wins such an acceptance it will be on the basis of rational persuasion, and perhaps he may fail to put theology's case persuasively enough, or else his hearers may not wish to be persuaded by any argument even if it is adequate. But at least the theologian must contend strenuously for the opportunity to state the case for the autonomy of his discipline and not to have this case prejudged.

Thus the present study, working within the perspective of theological thought, seeks to establish a possible interpretation of words and how we use them. It seeks to achieve that end in order that words may be seen to stand

11

in relation to the divine Word, the living Word of God, which is the proper subject of theology. I shall begin by considering contemporary philosophical estimates of language and the particular concerns evident in these. For theology and philosophy constantly interact. Philosophy, reflecting as it does more directly and visibly than theology the impact of man's changing cultural situation, brings to the fore new configurations of thought and new ways of speaking about human problems. Theology, therefore, is affected by philosophic currents and draws from philosophy much of its terminology. At the very least it cannot ignore what is going on in the philosophic realm. Philosophy poses human problems that are partly theology's problems too.

Yet there is an additional reason for theologians to be concerned over the way in which philosophers develop their concepts. Philosophy frequently spills over onto the territory of theology, for it claims to have something to say not only about the human but also about the divine — about the nature and reality (or unreality) of religious experience and about the existence (or nonexistence) of God, the object of that experience. That is why the theologian in dialogue with the philosopher can never simply accept the latter's conclusions and use them as a starting-point for his own constructions. For he has to make sure first that the philosopher's style of reasoning is not one that has tacitly chosen some particular theological option to the exclusion of others. This is where it becomes imperative for theology to assert its proper autonomy. And so, in my survey of philosophical theories of language, I shall scrutinize these theories in order to uncover their theological assumptions.

Once again, I would emphasize that such a course does not put thinking in bonds or demand a special privilege for Christian theology. Rather, it supposes that, when a philosopher makes statements that are properly theological or contain implicit theological choices, he should recognize the fact and not assert that he is speaking wholly from within the boundaries of his own discipline. Since there can be no theology without a faith-commitment, it is absolutely essential that any such commitment should not remain hidden or be stated ambiguously but should be recognized and laid clearly on the line.

I shall argue, indeed, that present-day philosophy asks us to endorse theories of language requiring faith-commitments other than that of the historic Christian faith and incompatible with the basis of Christian theology. Moreover, the deep chasm between opposing schools of thought concerning the nature of words and their relation to reality points to a situation of unease in which Christian theology can speak with healing effect. To grasp either horn of the dilemma with which we are confronted at the moment because of the split mind of modern philosophy would be too easy a way out; for it would be to declare a partisan allegiance. To hope to patch over the split through the mediation of an eclectic spirit would be to take the situation less than seriously. We need to consider each approach to the problem of language and find the theological foundation upon which it rests. Only then can the conflict of opposing viewpoints be understood and the positive contributions of seemingly contradictory theories concerning the function of words in human existence be brought to light.

Inherent in this procedure, naturally, is the belief that philosophy and theology can enter into dialogue while maintaining their distinct identities and their full right to flourish as separate disciplines. Neither need challenge the integrity of the other, while both may admit that independence does not deny interrelatedness. But the condition of mutual respect does require admitting the possibility that the traffic between them does not run on a one-way street. If theology can be informed by the findings of philosophy, then philosophy can be illuminated by the convictions of theology.

My analysis of the current "language situation" is preparatory only. That is to say that it is perfunctory and half-hearted — a kind of polite gesture in the direction of philosophy preliminary to getting down to the real issues. Philosophic insight into the use of words provides material that is not casual or expendable. It can go far to show us, for example, what religious language must be and how such language differs from the secular employ-

13

ment of words. But since my study is directed to relating human words to the divine Word, the nub of my argument comes when the confession made by Christian theology concerning the authenticity of God's self-revelation is applied to the understanding of language generally — and to the words of Scripture in particular. Christian hermeneutics, the interpretation of the Word of God, is the goal towards which my investigation is directed. My hope is, if not to reach that goal fully, yet to approach it by clearing the ground somewhat. The approach will be largely through defining the areas of crucial importance for the hermeneutical task.

To this latter end, the categories of *existence* and *history* will be considered as providing the necessary framework within which a theological estimate of language must function. And then, moving in more closely to my subject, I shall examine the theological perspective on *image, symbol,* and *myth.* On this basis I shall try to explain how Christian theology is able to use words in the service of the Word, and how the theological task arises out of the assurance of Christian faith concerning the Word of God heard in human language, authentically addressing men here and now.

Chapter 1

Language and Existence

CONSIDERED AS A HUMAN ART, LANGUAGE IS UNI-versal. Only *homo loquens* — man having words at his disposal — is truly man; and indeed, while there are communities known to lack other arts, none has been discovered lacking the art of speech.

Yet language is more than art, for it is also the basis of all science. It is the *sine qua non* of all consciously held knowledge. Language relates us to reality, allowing us to know what is there to be known in such a way that we can move in the human spheres of both theory and practice, thought and action. Because we can converse with one another, we are made aware of a common world in which we exist and to which we react. We come to recognize that we are warmed by the same sun and moved by the same affections. Common understanding of that which is outside of us and within us is brought to realization through common speech.

While every individual understands this truth on the basis of his own personal life-history of gaining mastery over words — and thus finding entrance into a word-using community — an exceptional life-history can occasionally drive the truth home with impressive force. Helen Keller, deprived of both sight and hearing, has recorded how the discovery that each thing has its own name opened for her the door to a meaningful universe and brought her into the full dimension of community. Out of her early experience of deprivation was born an unusual sensitivity to the human condition, as well as an intense appreciation of the function of language in human existence.

The example of Helen Keller helps us understand why we cannot really know anything until we know that we know it; and how our knowledge is established through the construction of a world of symbols giving concrete form to the world of our awareness. In a small way, each one of us witnesses to the essentiality of verbal symbolism whenever we remark, "I can't quite put into words exactly what I mean." By making this confession we are not simply apologizing for our failure to communicate, for we are also admitting to an area of uncertainty within ourselves. Unable fully to articulate what our thoughts are, we become conscious of a penumbra of indetermination in our thought processes themselves. We are stammering in our thinking, uneasy in our awareness of not being fully master in our own house. Once we know what it is we really want to say, we shall find the words in which to say it; or, more exactly, the words that we use will give us control over the direction of our ideas. So we frequently find it necessary to interlard our conversation with such phrases as "let me put it this way . . ." or "on second thought. . . ."

Human speech, then, is intimately bound up with the horizons of human existence and how these are enlarged. The comment, "I've never heard it put just like that before," is one ostensibly concerned with the form of words used; yet it is actually concerned with the substance of that which the words refer to. We grope for words and appropriate expressions whenever we are thinking strenuously; and, equally, we are apt to suspect the over-glib talker of being either a superficial or else a dishonest thinker. Each man dips into the common stock of words and makes his particular selection, one that depends on the social context of his existence and yet is unique to himself. If his contribution is found to be significant, it may affect the style and direction of speech used by others and thus help to bring about new perspectives of thought.

This is why language itself is never static. It is always changing with changes in human consciousness. At the same time, linguistic changes are gradual; for anything else would destroy the possibility for language to function as a medium of communication. New words are formed with reference to words already in existence, and old words are given new connotations. Sometimes the innovations are deliberate, as when individuals coin new words or embark upon "prescriptive definitions," experiments in word usage that, if they prove to be useful, are subsequently taken up into general speech. More often they arrive as though by stealth, and are already established before they are noticed. Words may readily be transformed completely in meaning. Thus the word *let* has come to signify *allow* instead of *hinder,* and the word *prevent* today stands for *disallow* in place of *go before.* But, whether the process of transformation takes centuries to evolve or is fairly abrupt, it happens so as not to disrupt everyday speech, and it happens in a context in which other words retain their traditional meanings. Linguistic change is controlled at every moment by linguistic continuity. If it were not so, we should be as frustrated as was Alice in *Through the Looking Glass* when she tried to talk to Humpty Dumpty, who insisted that words meant only what he decided they should mean. And even Humpty Dumpty kept intact the framework of English sentence structure, limiting his arbitrary meanings chiefly to nouns.

The fact that words have to be both stable and fluid in order to serve human purposes points to the fundamental duality of language, the exploration of which will be one of my main concerns throughout the course of my investigation. Stability is required because language gives us access to a public world that we do not ourselves bring into existence, a world that is no mere phantasmagoria, a world that has its own structures to which our thought must conform. The actuality of this world is presented to us along with the actuality of our own existence; and we deny it only at the cost of declaring all existence in time and space — our own and that of the whole universe around us — to be unreal. If things really exist in themselves and are more than the products of our thinking, then it follows that the words we use to describe them have to point to and mirror their independent reality. The structure of the actual world and the elements of that structure

17

are what our words must endeavor to represent as accurately as possible. Clarity and precision necessarily become the prime requirements of language, so that our speech will not distort what actually *is there* to be known. New words are needed, indeed, as new facts about the universe come within our purview; and our methods of making statements have to be progressively refined in order to permit ambiguities and linguistic muddles to be removed. All changes in language that do not contribute to the process of the more exact communication of factual truths and their logical relations are undesirable. The ideal of language pursued here is one in which every word functions as a univocal sign.

Reality, however, is more than the public world that can be observed and reported in objective terms. We cannot know anything about the public world unless we discover it to have some connection with our private experience. And this experience is always in flux. The fluidity of language reflects the language situation where all speech is not simply speech *about* objects but is also speech *by* subjects, subjects who use words to speak about their existence as they understand it from within. Here — with the subject and his private world (or rather, the public world seen in his private perspective) — is where language very possibly begins. Most often the individual who uses language is not concerned primarily with clarity, but rather with expressiveness. What matters is that he says what he wishes to express — somehow. It is not necessary that the words be exact, so long as they convey the intended meaning. Even should they be so oddly unusual that they communicate nothing intelligible to most people, the purpose of uttering or writing them will be achieved, provided that these words are understood by a few and perhaps by a single person alone. And since opportunities for new experiences are unlimited, expressive language cannot be contained within the bounds of previous usage. It is essentially open and continually changing.

The subjective dimension of language is of immense importance to us all the time, constituting our most immediate as well as our most widely used types of communication. In everyday speech the description of objects as such, or of any objective state of affairs, plays a relatively small part. We open our mouths in order to make requests, give orders, bestow praise or blame, indicate assent or dissent, communicate our opinions or elicit those of others, explain our feelings, complain, exhort, mock, admire, tease, and use words that are mere ejaculations conveying no information at all except the intensity of some emotion or bodily sensation.

How little ordinary language has to do with objective description can be seen from the testimony given by witnesses in a court of law. Even well-educated and highly articulate men and women, fully aware of what constitutes legal evidence and therefore of the kind of statements expected of them, find it difficult to keep their speech within the limits of the factual "objectivity" that the law requires. Since we view events from the angle of how they happen to affect our private consciousness, the effort to detach "what actually happened" from the impressions we received (because we were prepared to receive them) must always be a nearly impossible one. Of course, if we have special training we may do better than others; and here experience in giving testimony will be the best training, that is, *language* training. We are most *im*pressed by that which we have learned to *ex*press.

The truth that some witnesses in court have no intention of making their words express "what actually happened," and that they can diverge from objective fact either by deliberate falsification or else by presenting evidence selectively in order to give a misleading "impression," is very relevant to the consideration of language on its subjective side. The cynic holds that man has developed language in order to conceal his thoughts. Lying is morally reprehensible in the context of the objective dimension of language. It expresses (in the term used by Swift's rational horses in the fourth part of *Gulliver's Travels*) *the thing which is not.* Yet, in the subjective dimension of language, *the thing which is not* is an imaginative possibility, and thus the foundation of all human inventiveness as well as condition of all literary creation. Deliberately telling lies in order to deceive attacks the very nature of language, which is to communicate reality. Imagining non-actual states of affairs, on the other hand, is a triumph possible alone to *homo loquens,* whose intelligence is set free to use words for another purpose than that of describing matters of fact for which he has present evidence and which he can verify by means of objective criteria.

The most basic indication of the intrinsic importance of the subjective dimension of language is, of course, the multiplicity of languages. *Homo loquens* everywhere speaks, but speaking men do not necessarily understand one another. Words, which make possible communication above a rudimentary level, also raise barriers to communication. Insofar as every language is in principle learnable by those who do not know it, while in addition translation from one language into others is itself a language skill, the barrier of the unknown tongue is not entirely insuperable. At the present time translation by machines is widely used for international communication between scientists. Yet the thought that all language barriers may be swept away in time by our technological skill is probably illusory. The scientific use of language concentrates upon the objective dimension, and here the univocal sign rather than the expressive symbol controls the use of words. There is a real sense in which neither ordinary conversation nor imaginative literature can be translated at all, in that every translation even by a skillful and sensitive translator must be no more than a paraphrase of the original. Indeed, few authors have been able to produce literature of high worth in more than one language. The achievements of a Conrad, a Nabokov, or a Beckett stand out as exceptional; for what is aptly called our *mother tongue* is the womb in which our subjective consciousness has been formed. The duality of language here manifests itself most strikingly. The multiplicity of languages is something that we must wish away for the sake of community in understanding among all men; yet we cannot simply abandon diversity for the sake of unity, for that would be to renounce the most effective means of communication as yet achieved by men.

So far I have indicated in general terms the duality of language and how this hinges upon the objective and subjective faces of existence. It is time now to turn to a more specific examination of the two uses of words. I shall first inquire into the objective sphere, and how language has been regarded in the empirical stream of philosophy, a tradition that is concerned to direct language to the environing world.

The Empirical Perspective on Language

The Bible points to the dignity and preeminence of *homo loquens* when it describes Adam's naming of the animals in Eden. This act is not just Adam's own decision; for God Himself brings all creatures to Adam to see what he will call them, and He endorses Adam's choice (Gen. 2:19). Thus the use of words for coming to know external nature is specifically recognized in Scripture as one of the God-given powers of mankind. It is an original gift intended to show Adam's lordship over the earth within the good order of creation.

Then, after the Fall and mankind's progressive deterioration, comes the confusion of tongues at Babel. Unwilling to be God's stewards in the world, men wish to climb up to heaven in order to gain unlimited prestige for themselves (Gen. 11:4). But God confounds their pretensions by bringing about an alteration in their command over words. Man after Babel is still *homo loquens*. He is not denied the power of the word bestowed upon Adam in the Garden. But language now becomes ambiguous. What should unite the human race now divides it into races separated by the barrier of alien tongues. Brothers have turned into *foreigners*. The power of the word that is the power to know, and therefore to form plans and carry those plans into action, has been grievously weakened. And with the fragmentation of human speech comes a distortion of its essential character. Fallen man is no longer capable of maintaining the right relation between knowing subject and known object, which the original gift of language made possible. It is no longer the case, as it was in Eden, that what things are called is, in truth, their right name. *Logomachy* — dispute over words — is the heritage of Babel.

Thematically the story of Babel presents the predicament of language as we know it. From time to time thinkers have envisaged the possibility of overcoming the confusion of tongues by the deliberate creation of a universal language. In the seventeenth century the philosopher Leibniz proposed such a step as part of his plan for a total rational reconciliation of humanity's divisions; and his hope has been revived many times since. But its fulfilment has not come. Each effort to reverse Babel by an artificially contrived universal language (such as Esperanto, which earlier in this century aroused great enthusiasm) simply adds one more tongue to the rest.

The empirical tradition in philosophy tends to imagine that the root of the problem lies in the existence of language itself and that, because language obstructs our encounter with external reality fully as much as it serves as a means of recording this encounter, somehow it must be surpassed. We cannot do without it, certainly, yet we must so tame it that it will cease to mislead us. Regarding words with at least as much distaste as affection, the empiricist resembles Humpty Dumpty in his attitude towards them. He asserts that the whole question of using them is the question of who is to be master.

Thus, in classical times, Sextus Empiricus denied that the syllogism gives us any knowledge. He also argued that all attempts to speak about such verbal entities as God or Providence lead us into insoluble contradictions. At the beginning of the modern period Thomas Hobbes observed, "Words are wise men's counters, they do but reckon with them, but they are the money of fools." David Hume doubted the possibility of attaching any meaning to all words that did not arise out of sense impressions. And with John Stuart Mill there appears the distinction between real and merely verbal propositions.

However, the radical criticism of language that has blossomed in our own day is to be traced to G. E. Moore and to Bertrand Russell. Moore believed that most philosophical problems arise out of linguistic muddles. Russell turned to investigating how the grammatical form of sentences obscured their logical form, so that the philosopher's task was to reformulate statements in order to allow the logical form to stand out unambiguously. Empirical linguistic philosophy as a self-conscious "school" has its origins in the Cambridge of Moore and Russell, but more specifically with the publication in 1921 of Ludwig Wittgenstein's *Tractatus Logico-Philosophicus*.[1] There Wittgenstein declared:

> Language disguises thought. So much so, that from the outward form of the clothing it is impossible to infer the form of the thought beneath it, because the outward form of the clothing is not designed to reveal the form of the body, but for entirely different purposes.
>
> The tacit conventions on which the understanding of everyday language depends are enormously complicated.[2]
>
> All philosophy is a "critique of language."[3]

He therefore proposed for philosophy's essential task the examination of language in order to clarify propositions.[4] Since he spoke as though all propositions were statements in the natural sciences — dismissing all "metaphysical" statements as lying outside the limits of language[5] — he cleared the way for logical positivism. According to the logical positivists the "meaning" of any proposition is exhausted in its capacity for being empirically verified by the methods

---

[1] The title appeared with the first English edition of 1922. Russell supplied a preface for this edition, and pointed out in it how Wittgenstein's views had been developed in opposition to his own. Wittgenstein was a student of Russell's at Cambridge, later returning there as a Fellow of Trinity College and, after Moore's retirement, as one of the professors of philosophy in the university. Wittgenstein's own preface (dated 1918) acknowledges a debt to Russell and also to Gottlob Frege, a philosopher who sought to reduce arithmetic to logic. Quotations from the *Tractatus* are taken from the new translation by D. F. Pears and B. F. McGuinness (London: Routledge & Kegan Paul, 1961; New York: The Humanities Press). In this edition, as in that of 1922, the original German text is printed on the left-hand pages and the English translation on the right-hand pages. Numerals refer to the Propositions under which the argument of the *Tractatus* is arranged.

[2] *Tractatus*, 4.002, p. 37.

[3] *Ibid.*, 4.0031, p. 37.

[4] Wittgenstein comments in this connection that "it was Russell who performed the service of showing that the apparent logical form of a proposition need not be its real one" (*ibid.*, 4.0031, p. 37).

[5] See *ibid.*, 5.633, p. 117; 6.53, p. 151.

of the natural sciences. Any statements incapable of being so verified are "nonsense."[6]

Logical positivism became well known even beyond academic philosophical circles through A. J. Ayer's brilliantly polemical book *Language, Truth and Logic,* published in 1936. In that work Ayer went out of his way to include all theological language (as well as ethical language) under the heading of "nonsense." The result was that theologians and others who wished to find room for religious faith in their *Weltanschauung* reacted defensively. They sought to justify the language of faith within the limits they believed linguistic philosophy to have laid down. Some argued that theology could become wholly empirical by jettisoning all metaphysical notions (such as the word "God") and by concentrating upon the observable effects of religious faith upon the believer. This was the path taken by R. B. Braithwaite in his Eddington Lecture *An Empiricist's View of the Nature of Religious Belief,* and later by Paul van Buren in *The Secular Meaning of the Gospel.* The latter assumed that this was the sole road open to the Christian who was also a fully "contemporary" man. Others took comfort from the change in Wittgenstein's thought evidenced in the posthumously published *Philosophical Investigations.* There Wittgenstein spoke of various "language games," each coming under a different set of rules. So it could be argued, as Ian T. Ramsey has done,[7] that religious faith uses a linguistically "odd" kind of speech, one issuing in a "disclosure" of meaning for the believer that does not add to his empirical

---

[6] Logical propositions are exempted from this ban, but only because *they do not tell us anything.* The logical positivists found this explanation of logical statements in the *Tractatus.* There Wittgenstein wrote, "The propositions of logic are tautologies. Therefore the propositions of logic say nothing. (They are the analytic propositions.) ... One can calculate whether a proposition belongs to logic by calculating the logical properties of the *symbol.* And this is what we do when we 'prove' a logical proposition. For, without bothering about sense or meaning, we construct the logical proposition out of others using only *rules that deal with signs*" (*ibid.,* 6.1, p. 121; 6.11, p. 121; 6.126, p. 129; italics in the text). It is interesting to note that Russell, although he accepted Wittgenstein's view that logical propositions are tautologies, rejected logical positivism.

[7] *Religious Language, An Empirical Placing of Theological Phrases.*

knowledge but enables him to see it in a different light. Or it might be suggested that religious speech does not traffic in propositions, but rather in commands, promises, and exhortation.[8]

Now, it seems to me that all such defensive reactions are fundamentally mistaken. They assume a frame — less or more restrictive as the case may be — within which theology is to carry out its work. Empirical philosophers, of course, have every right to make an empirical critique of religious language; for they assume that religion itself must be subject to empirical criteria, since it can have no other reality than that which their philosophical presuppositions are prepared to allow it to have. But theologians who take their stand upon the reality of the Christian faith have, in point of fact, broken through the barriers erected by empiricism. They *begin* with the assumption that the Christian gospel makes sense, and so that theological speech is a legitimate enterprise. Therefore all attempts to fit "God-Talk" into the empirical frame of reference by those who explicitly confess adherence to a Christian perspective display the marks of desperation seen in the attempt to pour a quart of milk into a pint container. Either the milk overflows, or else another container, holding a quart but marked "One Pint," has been substituted surreptitiously. As I see it, the second technique is the one most often used. While some "analytic" restatements of theological language seriously compromise the integrity of Christian faith, it is empiricism chiefly that is silently repudiated. Theology must speak about *theos* —

---

[8] Willem F. Zuurdeeg opens his *An Analytical Philosophy of Religion* with the sentence: "If one adheres to the conception of philosophy as an analysis of language, the first step to be taken is to distinguish between various realms of discourse" (p. 23). Zuurdeeg takes language about religion to be essentially *convictional* language. Donald Evans' *The Logic of Self-Involvement* draws on the work of the Oxford linguistic philosopher J. L. Austin for his examination of theological speech as *performative utterances*. Robert W. Jenson's *The Knowledge of Things Hoped For: The Sense of Theological Discourse* couples British linguistic philosophy with European "new hermeneutic" and with the theology of hope, which sees human existence as "word-event." Jenson writes, "If we are to speak of God, let us remember: We will be commanding, blessing, cursing, complimenting, and insulting our hearers" (p. 239).

God Almighty — if it is to speak at all. Whatever combination of words may be used to try to get around the
charge of importing a transempirical reality into the conversation, the theologian cannot ever cancel his starting-
point. Somewhere, somehow, his language will break the
empirical frame, assuming that "experience" embraces a
transcendent element that no empiricist — except in a
Pickwickian sense of that term — could possibly admit.[9]

The later Wittgenstein pronounced the verdict that "philosophy may in no way interfere with the actual use
of language; it can in the end only describe it."[10] Such
a declaration is of service to others besides empiricists.
For example, it should prevent panicky theologians from
jumping to the conclusion that the word "God" must necessarily be meaningless to contemporary man. At the same

---

[9] Wittgenstein drew the empirical boundary for language with
precision in the *Tractatus,* namely, on the "lower" side of the sense
of the world as a whole, as distinct from facts concerning the world.
"*How* things are in the world is a matter of complete indifference
for what is higher. God does not reveal himself *in* the world" (6.432,
p. 149; italics in the text). This sense of the world is what Wittgenstein calls *the mystical,* saying that anything of this order cannot
be put into words. The sense of the "I" that can encounter a "Thou"
is clearly of this order (cf. *Tractatus,* 5.631, 5.632, p. 117) — and it
is just here that Ian T. Ramsey would place the justification for
religious language. In his *Language, Logic and God,* Frederick
Ferré explicitly states that speech concerning God is "metaphysical,"
saying that theological speech "projects a model of immense respon-
sive significance" (p. 164), but that finding the best model must
always be a matter of individual choice. Dallas M. High has at-
tempted to use Wittgenstein's *Philosophical Investigations* as a starting-point for a theory of religious language in his *Language, Persons
and Belief: Studies in Wittgenstein's 'Philosophical Investigations' and
Religious Uses of Language.* Yet his conclusions about "giving rea-
sons" for religious belief contrast glaringly with what Wittgenstein
said on this topic as recorded in *L. Wittgenstein: Lectures and Conversations on Aesthetics, Psychology and Religious Belief,* edited by
Cyril Barrett. Jenson tries to argue that, on the hints given by Wittgenstein about the boundaries of a person's language being the boundaries of his world, we are justified in holding religious discourse to
be the imposing and acknowledging of a picture in terms of which
we value the world "and so come to speak of it" (*The Knowledge
of Things Hoped For,* pp. 127-30). He acknowledges that this is
almost certainly going against Wittgenstein's intention — "but let
us do so anyway."

[10] *Philosophical Investigations,* Part 1, par. 124, p. 49.

time, it gives no assurance concerning the question of the *basis* to be used for "describing" the use of language in theological discourse. Until they know exactly the criteria proposed, theologians would be ill-advised to allow philosophers to describe for them what theology is saying. That does not mean, either, that they must stop their ears to the opinions of linguistic philosophers and live in some kind of holy isolation completely insulated from "secular" opinion. The technique of the linguistic analysts for discovering lack of clarity in propositions may often be helpful, for theologians too have to work with language (and, I would add, specifically with propositions). Moreover, Wittgenstein's analogy of "language games," though it may have limitations that its more enthusiastic adherents are reluctant to consider, has solid value in directing our attention to the manifold uses of language, and hence to the grammar of faith-statements.[11] Yet the actual use of language in theology is a theological use, namely, to allow the transcendent, divine Word to be heard. And no philosophical conditions can be laid down *ab extra* for that.

The empirical conviction that language is more often than not an obstacle to our knowledge of reality has its uses. It is a healthy reminder that we still live in the age of Babel. Thus it directs us to be critical of the words we use, because language as a vehicle of thought has real limitations. We may well be misled by the forms of speech we use, even when we draw our words out of Holy Scripture. Here the linguistic analyst reminds us of the intellectual dimension of the truth that the Christian believer is aware of on the moral and religious levels: that

---

[11] It is possible that the current concern with language theory may revive interest in John Henry Newman's *An Essay in Aid of a Grammar of Assent*. This work of 1870 anticipates Bertrand Russell's remark that "the study of grammar, in my opinion, is capable of throwing far more light on philosophical questions than is commonly supposed by philosophers" (*The Principles of Mathematics*, p. 42). Newman's dictum that "faith is a principal of action" makes contact with J. L. Austin's view of the connection between words and deeds. (Wittgenstein in *Philosophical Investigations* made the statement, "Words are also deeds.") And Newman's "illative Sense" has a parallel in Ian T. Ramsey's notion of "discernment" that causes "the penny to drop."

27

God's thoughts are not our thoughts and that man all too easily takes upon himself the right to speak for God and to claim divine sanction for human formulations of the gospel message.

Nevertheless, empirical philosophy's presumption that God's Word is limited to that which can be verified — or even "described" — at the level of human experience is one before which Christian faith can never bow. The theologian, indeed, is by virtue of his membership in the believing community compelled to insist that the Word of God is not bound by any human limitations and cannot be judged by any humanly fabricated criteria. "Let God be true, but every man a liar" (Rom. 3:4) is the watchword of all Christian theology. Words may mislead, yet the Word breaks through all human utterance to effect the purpose of the God who sends it forth (Isa. 55:10-11). Without this conviction born of the Spirit of Truth who witnesses to the Word, theology would be mute and unable to testify to the incarnate Word. Theology dares to believe that its imperfect utterances can still proclaim the precious and ever-present reality of the Word of life.

I shall return to the question of theological language later in the present study. At the moment it is simply necessary to underline two points: first, how empirical philosophy serves to remind us that language often fails to fulfil its function of representing truthfully the real world that it seeks to make accessible to us through its symbolic representations; and second, how the theologian cannot accept for himself the empirical view of that which is to be counted as being the limits of the real. I shall now turn to look at that tradition in philosophy which takes another estimate of language altogether, because it sees "reality" in quite another dimension than that of facts within the environing world.

The Idealistic Perspective on Language

The empirical tradition in philosophy is afraid that language, instead of doing its proper work of describing what actualities there are to be known in the world about us, will all too readily beguile us into a shadow world of empty ideas. The idealistic tradition harbors an opposite fear. Idealists claim that it is a great perversion of language to use it merely denotively, since its purpose is to reveal to us transphenomenal reality. In this connection, over against Wittgenstein's aphorism *language disguises thought* this dictum of Martin Heidegger might well be set: *language is the clearing-concealing arrival of being itself.*[12]

While it would be anachronistic to project the empiricist-idealist debate as such back into classical times, we can nevertheless find certain links across the centuries. For example, Wittgenstein writes in the *Tractatus*, "To understand a proposition means to know what is the case if it is true."[13] This corresponds very strikingly to the place in Plato's *Theaetetus* where the proposal is made to define knowledge as "right judgment plus an account." In this dialogue Socrates rejects such a proposal, affirming that true knowledge must be knowledge that cannot be mistaken but must be immediately certain — that is, knowledge of the archetypal forms lying behind sense perception. And when Plato wishes to give the true meaning of a word, he seeks to show that the speaker is a person whose credentials show him to be in possession of a knowledge going beyond the fluctuating opinions of men. He does this very precisely in the *Symposium*. There various speakers expand on aspects of our experience commonly thought to correspond to the meaning of the word *love*. But when Socrates arises to speak, he does not give one more view competing with previous views. Instead he reports the teaching communicated to him by a prophetess concerning the real nature of love. This teaching claims to be a definitive statement, not simply of how love affects us, but of what love essentially is. Furthermore, Socrates ends his account only to have Alcibiades testify to the way in which the whole life of Socrates proves him to be the man of true wisdom who has the right to speak with authority on ultimate issues.

---

[12] Quoted in *The Later Heidegger and Theology*, edited by James M. Robinson and John B. Cobb, Jr., p. 50. The sentence is from Heidegger's "Letter on Humanism" in *Platons Lehre von der Wahrheit* (1947), also published separately as *Über den Humanismus* (1949).

[13] 4.024, p. 41.

For Plato man is capable of hearing the voice of truth itself and, in consequence, of speaking that which is true — or, as he says in the *Philebus*, of having true words written in his soul. Language is not in itself a barrier standing in the way of the truth, yet the words that we use in speech are at best only images of the truth. Thus in the *Cratylus* Socrates warns that knowledge is not to be derived from the study of names; and he adds that the fact that a multitude of names exist must not be allowed to mislead us into thinking that all things are in flux, as though nothing absolute existed in its own right. However, it is clear that Plato believed words to be dangerously misleading chiefly when they were deliberately misused. Hence his condemnation of the Sophists for manufacturing false images in order to lead men astray through treacherously enticing words.

Coming to the modern age, we find language providing Hegel with the starting-point for his exposition of absolute idealism. He argues that all words, if their meaning is pressed, can be seen to refer not to particular objects of sense perception but to general ideas; and, ultimately, all our ideas stand revealed as aspects of self-consciousness. The idealistic understanding of language's function — not to report precisely "what is the case" with reference to facts existing in their own right, but to disclose a nexus of "meaning" to our consciousness — is evident in Edmund Husserl's development of the phenomenological method. Husserl drives a decisive wedge between meaning and things, a procedure fully consistent with his positing of the transcendental ego that creates its own world.[14] The idealistic tradition, all the same, did not make the question of language as such a central issue until linguistic problems came to the fore in empirical thought. Concentration upon the role of language came with the effort to counter the "objectivizing" outlook of empiricism with its admiration for, and close ties with, scientific objectivity. The "later" Heidegger's preoccupation with *hermeneutics* and

---

[14] For more about the idealistic identification of "world" with human consciousness, see below, pp. 40-1. The connection between "meaning" and the subjective approach to reality is considered in more detail in Chapters 2 and 3. See below, pp. 54-7, 65-7.

his characterization of language as "the house of being" arose from this cause and from his belief that all true thinking must be "meditative thinking."

Twentieth-century existentialism from its beginnings has displayed the marks of being a disguised form of idealism — disguised because from the 1920s until quite recently Hegel and German idealism generally were unfashionable, and a wholly new label helped to lend intellectual respectability and the effect of novelty to this type of thinking. Heidegger's continual preoccupation with the question of metaphysics, his view that thought is Being disclosing itself in man and that language is Being's silence made vocal in man, shows idealism asserting itself very strongly. Until his recent philosophical "conversations" with Hegel, Heidegger was not accustomed to appeal to nineteenth-century German idealistic philosophers to support his view. Instead, he appealed most frequently to nineteenth-century Romantic poets, whose works reflect a similar outlook — though more ambiguously.

In the idealistic tradition Being is conceived as shining *through* the material world, yet incapable of taking residence *in* it. For Plato, man while dominated by sense impressions is a prisoner in a dark cave, watching shadows on its walls. The philosopher alone escapes to step into the daylight. Heidegger makes use of a similar metaphor in his essay "Conversation on a Country Path about Thinking."[15] There he speaks about seeking for man's nature by moving away from human "habitation." Just so, a walk away from houses into the darkness of the countryside at night makes the stars shine more brightly "because it nears their distances in the Heavens." For Heidegger, the "objectivizing" character of scientific thinking is destructive of man's true nature. It "beguiles" man (Heidegger's term), causing him to accept what Plato sees as shadows. Where Plato uses the dramatic image of escaping from an artificially illuminated cave, Heidegger uses a more naturalistic image, one of leaving behind the lights of houses and going out under the stars. Presumably, night is used as a symbol of Being, because, though it seems dark to those

---

[15] In *Discourse on Thinking*. A translation of *Gelassenheit* by John M. Anderson and E. Hans Freund.

who step out from their homes, it glows with an unfailing and eternal light. The seemingly tiny pinpoints of brightness in the sky gradually become illumination for our country path.

In both illustrations, the world of sense and merely human security must be left behind if one is to reach the world of reality and find the path to true self-knowledge.

As has been already noted, Heidegger characterizes language as the *clearing-concealing* arrival of Being. For the idealist, language necessarily has a dual nature. On the one hand, it misleads insofar as it is taken to be a means of knowing sensory phenomena and insofar as it is thought to refer primarily to the material world and to our life in it. On the other, it is our passport to the real world of thought lying beyond all images of sense. It becomes necessary for the idealist, on this account, to insist that language is not rightly used — or is used only in a trivial sense — when it serves merely as a complex of signs to guide us around the realm of actualities of "objectivizations." (This is what Plato characterized as trying to learn from images.) The proper use of language, rather, is to bring us away from the "habitations" of men into the luminous darkness of thought so that we may know transphenomenal truth. In this event, truth is not Wittgenstein's "knowing what the case is" with reference to things around us. It is truth in the classical sense of *aletheia*, which, as Heidegger never tires of saying, is the revealing or uncovering of Being.

Truth in this latter sense may be conceived to lie in concepts that, being themselves not conditioned by the limitations of time and space, lead us from the changing to the changeless, from the Many to the One. Or it may be conceived to be approached through language that, while *apparently* referring to our everyday world, *really* transcends sensory existence and brings us into contact with the intelligible and inconceivable world lying behind all sensory imaging. In other words, truth may be thought to be brought into our ken through the medium of the language of myth.

Plato envisages the task of the philosopher as ascending to dialectical thought, where the intelligence would rise free of the senses and deal wholly with the eternal Ideas. Yet, in order to grasp essential truth transcending our earthbound imaginations, Plato makes use of figurative stories or "myths." In the nineteenth century, Schelling found it necessary to pass from what he called the Negative Philosophy of Ideas to the Positive Philosophy embracing myth and religious revelation. A similar progress can be seen today in Heidegger with his espousal of the program of *going beyond* metaphysics. Heidegger now is saying that he wishes to write as a poet rather than as a philosopher. And he finds his philosophic texts chiefly in Greek myths and German romantic poetry, Hölderlin being one of his especial favorites. (This particular combination, incidentally, recalls strongly the outlook of the early Hegel. Although Hegel finally set himself up as the champion and interpreter of Christianity, he at first thought Christian faith to be a foreign intrusion, and held Greek religion to be much more in accord with the Germanic soul.)

Heidegger's voice is being heard today. At an International Colloquium on Heidegger's Conception of Language, held at Pennsylvania State University in September 1969, Heinrich Ott gave a paper entitled "Hermeneutical and Personal Structure of Language," in which he contrasts the two opposing approaches to language, which I have called the empirical and the idealistic. These he labels "the technological scientistic view of language" and "the speculative hermeneutical experience of language." In effect, he chooses the latter, taking Heidegger as his guide.

In speaking of the "scientistic" outlook as a *view* and of the "speculative" outlook as an *experience*, Ott provides evidence concerning the idealistic foundation of the latter. To an empiricist, man's capacity for speech suggests that he has access to words in much the same way that he has access to a bag of tools. (This comparison, by the way, is found in Wittgenstein.)[16] But an idealist sees man not so much using words as experiencing, through words, a realm beyond all verbal expression. The utilitarian aspect of speech is incidental; its power to illuminate man's total consciousness is essential. Thus Max Picard writes in his

---

[16] *Philosophical Investigations*, Part I, par. 11, p. 6.

book *Man and Language,* "Because language comes from an eternal world, man is able to reach out beyond himself through language." Similarly, Heidegger has adopted the term *hermeneutic* in connection with his theory of language because of its (possibly fanciful) derivation from Hermes, the messenger of the gods. As Hermes brought men news of their fate, so Heidegger imagines hermeneutic to be original "hearing" as well as interpretation. Through language man learns "Being's favor." In other words, speech is an intimation of verities beyond all imaging. It comes as a favor, a gift of Transcendent Reality, because we cannot control or direct it — it directs us.

Until recently empirical linguistic philosophy dominated the Anglo-Saxon world, and so theologians widely sought to enter into dialogue with this type of thinking. There are signs that the magnetism of the empirical mode is waning, perhaps because of the unspectacular nature of the results achieved, and that the "speculative" approach is being again seriously considered.[17]

---

[17] Until his death in 1965 Paul Tillich was an influential interpreter of the German idealistic tradition to the North American and British publics. But he stood as a lone figure, and left behind no clearly identifiable "school." Heidegger's linguistic thinking has penetrated the English-speaking world only to a limited extent, although it has received some attention, notably in the first two volumes of the series "New Frontiers in Theology: Discussions Among German and American Theologians" edited by James M. Robinson and John B. Cobb, Jr.: *The Later Heidegger and Theology* and *The New Hermeneutic.* Meanwhile, the sixties have seen a strong revival of natural theology — which was under a cloud during the ascendency of so-called neo-orthodoxy — especially in connection with process philosophy, and there has been a renewed interest in metaphysical thinking in general.

An interesting indication of current trends is to be found in Langdon Gilkey's *Naming the Whirlwind: The Renewal of God-Language.* Gilkey voices dissatisfaction with the narrowness of the empirical and the "secularist" viewpoints, arguing for the need to reinstate both Christian theological language and the language of speculative metaphysics. He builds his case on the concept of *experience.* We must find, he says, "those dimensions or regions of ordinary experience to which the language of religious symbols has reference, and so in terms of which such symbols can be said to have legitimate meaning and real possibility" (p. 20). He finds such dimensions, in Tillichian fashion, in the penumbra of "ultimacy" surrounding all human experience. Such "deeper" regions of experience can be described only symbolically. In other words, the ideal-

The idealistic or "speculative" approach to language certainly is hospitable to *God-talk,* if by such a term is meant reference to a transcendent dimension of human experience. It supposes — indeed demands — an eternal "Word" giving truth and meaning to all human words. Yet it also insists that all *God-talk* has only symbolic value, since what is experienced is in essence ineffable. Therefore it also binds theologians to the dogma that the "Word" is immanent in language to the extent that language escapes from spatial and temporal limitations and leaves behind the phenomenal world.

Max Picard, for example, asserts that man "encounters within himself a zone beyond the realm of language." He continues: "This divine element in man responds to all the things that are unspeakable and in the moment of response man is set back behind his own existence which is determined by Logos."[18] The Fall, according to Picard, is constituted by man's inability to rise in the power of that divine element to the eternal. The result is the dissolution of the primal unity of language and the poverty of language as we know it. Our talk has become wholly bound up with our sensory existence.

The idealist, in the last resort, denies the possibility of a revelation of the "Word" that is not mediated through "the divine element in man."[19] He finds foolish the notion that God condescended to make Himself known *in* the world, or *in* words that have not first been purged of everything worldly so as to shine through the darkness with a light that this world fails to see. It follows, therefore, that the theologian who adopts the idealistic interpretation of language must inevitably find himself in a

istic concept of language is invoked. John Macquarrie's *God-Talk: An Examination of the Language and Logic of Theology* argues that theological language is basically "existential-ontological." Mac-Quarrie concludes by saying that Heidegger's movement from existential to ontological language "constitutes a kind of paradigm or prototype for the language of theology" (p. 247).

[18] *Man and Language,* pp. 16-17.

[19] In *The Spirit of Christianity* Hegel wrote: "Hence faith in the divine grows out of the divinity of the believer's own nature; only a modification of the Godhead can know the Godhead" (*On Christianity: Early Theological Writings by Friedrich Hegel,* translated by T. M. Knox, p. 266).

position where he is unable to proclaim the Christian message of the Word made flesh, even should he intend most sincerely to do this.

The example of Rudolf Bultmann illustrates how such an eventuality comes about.

Rudolf Bultmann's Hermeneutic

Bultmann's New Testament hermeneutic, as is well known, issues from a *missionary* motive. Bultmann wishes to make the Christian gospel understandable to men of today, and he undertakes to do so by removing accidental stumbling blocks to its reception. These obstacles have arisen, he believes, through the difference between the world-view of the first century and that of the twentieth. To us, the language of the New Testament reflects a mythical picture of the universe, which the advent of scientific knowledge has proved to be untenable. However, the images in which the New Testament writers presented the gospel have no essential connection with the gospel itself, which is a direct challenge to man to receive the Word of God in his personal existence. Once the accidental forms in which the gospel used to be clothed have been removed, its essence will stand forth unambiguously. *Then* the necessary and unremovable stumbling block to the reception of the gospel will stand forth undisguised by outmoded language. The perennial truth of the gospel demands that man hear the Word as God's own Word and submit to it by an act of the will.

Because Bultmann wishes to accomplish his end of letting the gospel proclaim itself in all its purity by means of the expedient of "demythologizing," it might be thought that he has no use at all for myth. Are not the presuppositions of his position very much those of a nineteenth-century empirical thinker, of some positivist of the lineage of Comte who sees no value in prescientific cosmologies or ontologies and who wishes to stay within the limits of naturalistic thinking?

This seemingly plausible viewpoint is shattered by the fact that the biblical record is absolutely essential for Bultmann. His whole work is dependent upon it, and his message of God acting upon us and granting us authentic existence issues from it. The Bible provides us with the language of salvation, however much we may wish to re-interpret that language. What Bultmann insists upon is that the *words* of Scripture must be demythologized before they can be meaningful to us, even though the original writers and readers of those same words took them lit-erally. Therefore, it is out of mythological words that the Word comes; and we see how it comes when we demy-thologize. The objective reference of the individual state-ments made in words evaporates at this point. What re-mains is the transphenomenal reality that cannot be caught in terms belonging to our time and our space. Truth shines *through* the words of the gospel story; it cannot, properly speaking, be found *in* them. Faith, not assent to proposi-tions couched in mythical language, is what is required of us. And faith is not capable of being objectivized. It is a living *(existentiell)* commitment to and trust in God himself.

The possibility of faith, says Bultmann in his essay "The Word of God in the New Testament," lies in man's own existence. The crucial question is whether man "is willing to understand the Word, which confronts him here and now, as God's Word."[20] On the face of it, this statement sounds unexceptionable. What is this Word, though, and who is the God who acts upon us by His Word? Bultmann understands by the Word not the histor-ical figure of Jesus but the understanding-event that he calls the *kerygma*. "Jesus Christ confronts men in the kerygma and nowhere else."[21] The Word has no temporal anchorage except that *through* historical time as a con-tinuity of human understanding. It has no essential link with anything that may have happened on earth. "There-fore," says Bultmann, "nothing needs to be taught about Jesus except . . . *that* in his historical life the event had its beginning and the event continued in the preaching of the community."[22]

Bultmann has italicized the *that* in the above quota-tion. Here we may be reminded, perhaps, of Schelling's

---

[20] *Faith and Understanding*, I, 301.
[21] *Ibid.*, pp. 310-11.
[22] *Ibid.*

basing his Positive Philosophy upon the concept of God as "a pure That." (Bultmann, of course, does not draw his ideas from Schelling. The parallel is one of a similar mode of thinking, not one of conscious reference.) But the important point is that Bultmann should take for granted that the event which reveals the Word of God is a spiritual "breaking through" into our consciousness, and is independent of any specific happening in history — it simply displays itself there in its timeless authenticity. It must be something within the unchanging human consciousness (in Picard's terminology "the divine element in man") that recognizes this event and carries it through the continuing consciousness of the Christian community, finding the suprahistorical *that* to be present where the kerygma is proclaimed.[23]

Similarly, while Bultmann speaks about *God* as though he means the personal Being named in Scripture, *God* is for him a way of viewing our mode of being. Thus, in the essay "What Does It Mean to Speak of God?" he explains that "to apprehend our existence is to apprehend God."[24] Again, in a recent essay on "The Idea of God and Modern Man," he says that the phrase "encounter with God" must be understood to refer to "the readiness

---

[23] Although Bultmann's dehistoricizing of Jesus has received much attention, it has been mostly overlooked that the correlative of this must inevitably be the dehistoricizing of the individual who receives the Word that is not to be found within history. Heinz Zahrnt comes close to the matter in *The Question of God: Protestant Theology in the Twentieth Century,* when he remarks that Bultmann's theology fails to do justice to the fact "that the human person is also a man who possesses not merely a mind, but also a heart and a body" (p. 245). Zahrnt, however, does not follow through this thought, except to reproach Bultmann for concentrating upon the individual and neglecting society. Yet what is most evident is that Bultmann effectively abolishes not merely the social outreach of the individual but the existing individual himself. However much he may speak about him, he has cut the link with history that gives the individual his unique and personal existence. Only a disembodied consciousness can receive a Word that has no rootage in the world of specific happenings.

[24] *Ibid.,* p. 63. The idealistic overtones of such a statement are very plain, indicating as it does that the coming to consciousness of the fact of its own "imprisonment" in space and time makes the soul realize its essential participation in the divine and eternal.

for the eternal to encounter us at any time in the present
... in openness in allowing something really to encounter
us that does not leave the I alone."[25] The upshot of Bultmann's refusal to admit "objectivizing" or "mythical" language about God is that the word *God* becomes the equiva-
lent of the sense of the eternal impinging upon the temporal, the grounding of the phenomenal *I* in a transphenomenal reality.

In other words, Bultmann has shut himself securely
inside the idealistic box. Karl Barth is surely right when
in his criticism of Bultmann, "Rudolf Bultmann — an Attempt to Understand Him," he places the weight of his
criticism upon Bultmann's acceptance of the hermeneutical
principle of *pre-understanding*. Before he reads Scripture,
Bultmann has already decided what is there to be understood. He knows who God is, what encounter with God
means, and what is involved in the act of faith. Therefore,
says Barth, Bultmann's prejudging of what the reality of
the situation must be leaves no place for the Holy Spirit,
who alone can open to us the Scriptures and reveal them
to us as testimony to the Word of God.[26]

Bultmann, asserting dogmatically that to speak of God
is to speak about our existence, has gone on to make Heidegger's early analysis of existence the basis for his pre-
understanding of the biblical message. This is not accidental — although, of course, he might have chosen another
thinker of similar outlook — because in Bultmann's understanding of what it is to hear the Word we find the very
same elements of the idealistic view of language that are
to be found in Heidegger. And, indeed, although Bultmann
has chosen to ignore the later developments in Heidegger's
thinking about hermeneutics, some of these developments
make explicit what is latent in Bultmann's orientation to
words and the Word. As much as Heidegger, Bultmann
wishes to know the true nature of man. As much as Heidegger, he believes that such knowledge will come by
looking away from man the empirical individual to the

---

[25] Rudolf Bultmann, *et al., Translating Theology into the Modern Age*, p. 94.

[26] "Rudolf Bultmann — an Attempt to Understand Him," in *Kerygma and Myth*, II, 125-27.

eternal that shines through the temporal — or in Heidegger's terminology, to "that-which-regions" man. And, as much as Heidegger, who speaks of walking out into the darkness in order to find light, he finds faith to be the incommunicable truth about our existence on earth, which nevertheless *is* communicated when language ceases to be about objects and becomes, as it essentially is, the uncovering of Being.

For Heidegger the poets and their myths are the messengers of the gods, and in them language itself speaks. So, likewise, through the mythological language of the Bible we encounter the eternal within the temporal, according to Bultmann. But first we must *demythologize* this language; that is, we must become aware that the words of the Bible are not literally significant as words describing actual happenings. (With poetry, of course, such demythologizing is unnecessary; for we assume from the first that poets give us, not factual information, but insight into the human condition.) The language of the Bible, then, becomes meaningful when it speaks to our understanding of ourselves, allowing us to be "open" to the eternal dimension of the self beyond the individual ego.

Language itself speaks, says Heidegger, through man; man is the loudspeaker making audible the silent tolling of Being. Jesus in the Bible, in Bultmann's interpretation, takes over the function of representing man as Heidegger views man. Jesus, so Bultmann affirms, is the Word not because of anything in particular that He says but because He speaks for God. He is an "event." And that event is "brought about only in the words of men."[27]

Bultmann adds, ". . . and precisely in that human word which proclaims judgment and forgiveness." Yet, although he presses into service biblical phrases, Bultmann interprets these phrases after the idealistic pattern. When he speaks of *faith*, faith takes on a strong family likeness to Heidegger's *primal thinking*. His notion of *judgment and forgiveness* is very close to Heidegger's notion of *releasement*, i.e. an act of not-willing but accepting Being's favor.

In his introduction to Bultmann's *Faith and Understanding* Robert W. Funk says that critics misunderstand Bult-

---

[27] "The Word of God in the New Testament," p. 310.

man if they take his concept of self-understanding subjectively. Such misunderstanding would be avoided by
substituting *world* for *self-understanding*. Yet this is merely
to say that Bultmann's philosophical presupposition is objective idealism rather than subjective idealism. He assumes the eternal that man grasps through receiving the
Word to be the form of reality itself. The fundamental
theological objection to this presupposition remains. The
"world" to which the self-understanding consciousness gains
access is still not the actual world created by the Lord
of heaven and earth. The Word who is Jesus Christ is still
excluded from becoming flesh and tabernacling with man
on earth. Because this Word has nothing to do with the
"historical" Jesus it is a transphenomenal "event" that
flashes across history. As "spiritual" it cannot put down
roots in the earth. It cannot actually engage itself with
the world of men who individually live, work, suffer, hope,
and ask for their daily bread and the bread of life that
will nourish them now and eternally.

If the Word has not indeed descended to our human
level, He remains a docetic Christ, an "event" discernible
to our self-understanding in an idealistic "spiritual" world,
but not the Son of Man who has shared our infirmities
and taken away our sins. If the "historical" Jesus is irrelevant to the preaching of the kerygma, the kerygma is not
relevant to the whole man, but only to human self-consciousness. We have never known Immanuel, God with
us. Christ can be the Savior of the world only if He has
really entered the world, and not just the "world" constituted
by our self-understanding. The words of Gregory of Nazi-
anzus ring as true today as when he spoke them against
Apollinarius: "That which He has not assumed, He has
not healed."

The Word in Existence

My subject has been Language and Existence. So far
I have been dealing with theories of language that limit
existence by erecting a pre-understanding of what existence
must be. For the empiricist, existence is limited to sense-
experience in a world of objects, objects that subjects
attempt to come to know — and generally misrepresent

because language gets in between them and the objectively real sum of things. Contrariwise, for the idealist, language prevents existence from being dissolved into objects having no meaning and subjects having no being. Because each self-conscious subject participates in the power of language, he can understand what it is to have a "world." He can transcend the separateness of empirical existence and realize within his self-consciousness the original wholeness of ultimate reality, of Being where subject and object are not divided.

Empiricism, in its single-minded drive for objectivity on the level of sense-perception, is nonreligious. It secularizes the world by banishing from it every vestige of transcendence. If the consistent empiricist wishes to admit a place for religious experience, as the later Wittgenstein did, he can only, like Wittgenstein, refer to *the mystical* about which nothing can be said. All attempts to introduce a religious dimension into the empirical universe cheat. For they must assume that, at some point or other, the world of objects is entered by a transcendent Word that speaks out of the silence; and empiricism can never admit any such point without denying its own principles and admitting that subjects have access to a "world" defying empirical description.

Idealism is inherently religious. Speaking of the birth of classical philosophy, Werner Jaeger says, "Though philosophy means death to the old gods, it is itself religion."[28] When Plato "demythologized" the Homeric myths, he did so in the interests of a purer religious imagination. He did not deny the validity of the popular religious consciousness, but questioned its adequacy for representing the Divine in words. In the *Timaeus* Plato wrote: "But the father and maker of this universe is past finding out, and even if we found him to tell of him to all men would be impossible."

Turning to modern times, we can see how the motive behind Hegel's Absolute Idealism is to be found in his early theological writings. And his philosophy is hardly to be separated from his conviction that it established Christianity as the absolute religion — in spirit if not in letter. Heidegger

---

[28] *Theology of the Early Greek Philosophers*, p. 72.

drew on his training in a Jesuit seminary when he made hermeneutics the central concern of his philosophy. And, although in *Sein und Zeit* God appears only through his absence (because of the decay in the idea of transcendence that Heidegger found in the modern consciousness), he did not rest until he could announce that the gods were returning through the good offices of the poetic imagination.

The God of biblical faith, however, does not wait to be validated by any theory of existence; nor does He ever lack a messenger to announce His presence. He revealed Himself to Abram; He appointed His prophets to witness to His will for Israel; He came in His incarnate Word; and He announces Himself in the work and worship of His Church by the Holy Spirit. Thus theologians are not concerned to ask *whether* God is manifest in existence or in *what kind of world* (or self-understanding) the Word communicates meaningfully to man. They begin from God's own assurance that the Word He sends forth into the world does not return to Him empty, but accomplishes His purpose in the created world (Isa. 55:11). They begin with the datum of revelation, accepted on the authority of God Himself.

Nevertheless, theologians are aware that the Word of God's own revelation always reaches men in human words. And when they engage in the theological disciplines they themselves use human words and expect other human beings to understand what they say. They are existing individuals sharing the human condition with all its limitations, not privileged persons exempted from struggling with the continuing problems of existence, among which the problem of language and its interpretation is crucial. So they cannot escape into a private world, "doing their own thing" in isolation from other disciplines — and especially not in isolation from philosophy. Indeed, while the hermeneutical question is basic to theology in every age, it is the concentration of philosophers today upon the philosophy of language that has aroused theologians from their dogmatic slumbers to look at hermeneutics with renewed concern.

Empirical philosophy concentrates upon the objectivity of the given, reminding us that the "world" of which subjects are aware is inadequate unless it corresponds to what actually exists. And the theologian must agree, while dissenting to the restrictions of the empirical viewpoint. God is not God unless He is objectively real, and His existence cannot be circumscribed within a "world" of pure Being mediated by the self-consciousness of subjects and divorced from the world of actually existing things. The God of idealism cannot be the Creator of heaven and earth. On the other hand, the idealistic argument concerning the emptiness of objects apart from subjects that can be aware of a meaningful world is of immediate concern to theologians. God is not just another object among objects of which we can gain knowledge. We cannot know God as He is in Himself but only as He relates Himself to us, and therefore our subjectivity is necessarily involved in the discovery of God as Subject. Our words about Him take their reality from reflecting the divine Word which alone makes language meaningful.

My second lecture will take up the theme of the subjective interpretation of existence, and especially of the drive towards subjective meaning that displays itself in the creation and interpretation of myths. There I shall pursue further the question of language and existence as this question concerns the relationship of myth to history and so of religion — man's quest for the divine — to Christian faith, the response to the gospel of God's action in history.

Chapter 2

Myth, Mythic Patterns, and History

Nor LONG AGO, THE STUDY OF MYTH WAS LARGELY the preserve of anthropologists and historiographers of religion. Today myth is in the center of debate in a wide variety of areas: in philosophy, psychology, sociology, theology, literary criticism, and even politics. As one wit has put it, "Today we are all being myth-informed."

In the previous lecture the subject of myth came up within the context of reflection upon language. Now this subject moves into the center. As a starting-point (and without following him all the way), I shall draw upon the presentation of myth given by the neo-Kantian philosopher Ernst Cassirer.

Cassirer has suggested that the possession of intelligence by man, though important, is not man's decisive characteristic. What really distinguishes him from other animals is his ability to construct symbols that are subsequently pressed into the service of rational thought. Man is *animal rationale;* but chiefly he is *animal symbolicum.*[1] He does not first understand the world, and then learn how to put his knowledge into words. Rather his invention of verbal symbols provides the possibility of his having knowledge. The symbols he uses shape the way in which knowledge comes to him. Cassirer argues, therefore, that myth (as the primal form of thinking) and language go hand in hand in educating man to make sense of his existence. He writes,

[1] *An Essay on Man: An Introduction to a Philosophy of Human Culture,* p. 44.

45

"Like the spirit of language, the mythmaking genius 'has' separate and individualized forms only in so far as it 'posits' them, as it carves them out of the undifferentiated whole of its pristine vision."[2]

We can see how this is so, when we consider the logic of myth. It has been a perennial problem to students of myth that myths seem to be the embodiment of illogicality. They unite the most bizarre elements in the most unpredictable ways. Nevertheless, myths are always stories. The stories they tell are as wild and apparently as inconsequential as dreams. Yet that does not alter their meaningfulness; and, indeed, the community between dreams and myths has been a fruitful source of insight into the understanding of dreams. The point is that every story has its own form, its unique inner coherence. When a story is ended, we are conscious of the satisfaction of having learned something.

Very much the same satisfaction comes from the completion of a task that we have set ourselves, or from a journey safely over. For there is a teleological structure in a story — it is not simply one-thing-after-another. Moreover, the telling of the story establishes the certainty of this structure. Order has been won out of chaos through the power of the word. And, because the story can be told again and again, the victory is permanent. The flux of time seems to have been overcome. A slice of existence has been lifted up into eternity.

The *meaning* of a story, having been produced by means of words, is hardly to be detached from the words that created it. This fact must be clear to anyone who has had the experience of telling bedtime stories to children. How often the teller of the story is stopped abruptly because a single unimportant word has been omitted or changed in the telling. Here the point is that to the child the story is the total *pattern of words*. An adult who is used to regarding words as tools to work with becomes impatient

---

[2] *Myth and Language*, p. 14. In *The Burning Fountain: A Study in the Language of Symbolism*, Philip Wheelwright explains myth from much the same standpoint. He writes: "Myth, then, is not in the first instance a fiction imposed on one's already given world, but is a way of apprehending that world. Genuine myth is a matter of perspective first, invention second" (p. 150).

with such apparent concern over trifles. *He* thinks of the story as a mental construct, detachable from words. But the child regards the story as a living entity made out of words. He wants "his" story — not another one like it. A substitute will not do, any more than a strange dog of the same breed will console him if he happens to lose his pet. A change in words is a change of story, and when the recognized verbal order (which is the essence of the story) is violated, chaos threatens. Another way of putting the same point is that a sacred ritual has been profaned and turned into a commonplace action. The "magic" of the story loses its power when the telling ceases to be an incantation and becomes a mere chronicle of events.

Of course, the parallel between myth in primitive societies and children's stories cannot be pressed too far. The language-situations are extremely different, since today's child is introduced early to an instrumental, sign-use of language, which he is taught to regard as the "normal" one. Nevertheless, in growing up, each life reenacts in part the history of the human race. Children experience to some degree the formation of a meaningful world through the mythic power of language. The primitive inability to distinguish between the mythic world and the everyday world is a marked characteristic of young children. Their personal excursions into mythmaking frequently result in their being accused of being deliberate liars! The close relationship between the mythic and the religious consciousness is very visible here. It has been given expression, for example, in Wordsworth's ode "Intimations of Immortality from Recollections of Early Childhood." Wordsworth writes, "Heaven lies about us in our infancy! / Shades of the prison-house begin to close / upon the growing boy." Wordsworth's description of how "the vision splendid" in adulthood "fades into the common light of day" might be taken as an account of the change that overcomes language as it becomes restricted to empirical sign-language use.

Myth and Religion

I should like to turn now to the specific connection of myth with religion.

Myths are basically stories about the gods, that is, about the powers upon which man's continued existence is thought to depend absolutely. Cassirer points out that we know of no society in which there is not some concept of the secular existing as well as the sacred, even though religion dominates almost all aspects of primitive societies. But the important experiences of tribal living — and this is preeminently its means of livelihood — are governed by myth and ritual. Myth and ritual go together, because the point of knowing the gods is to take appropriate action in order to ensure (or compel) the availability of their power for men. Indeed, historical evidence points to the priority of ritual over myth. Symbolic action comes before symbol-structured story. Nevertheless, the two activities are intimately related. Naming the gods is also action. The concept of a *word-event* (which is so prominent a feature of the "new hermeneutic" in Germany today) applies precisely in primitive religions.

To know a name is to have power over the bearer of the name, be he god or fellow-creature. And Cassirer has gathered an impressive array of examples of religious belief, from different periods, concerning the power of the gods arising out of their ability to speak a particular sacred word. Some gods are actually said to have been brought into being through the uttering of a word or sacred incantation.

If we look at this belief from the point of view of language, the reason for it is clear. Before some thing has been given a name, it remains unknown. It does not emerge out of the undifferentiated background to existence. Naming it causes it to "be," in the sense that it now enters into human consciousness as an entity existing in its own right and having its own characteristic modes of behavior. There is therefore no distinction to be made between the name and the object named. The object *is* its name. Since the primary experience a primitive person has is of himself as an active agent, having specific powers and abilities in imposing his will upon his environment, he sees the world around him as alive with similar agents, whose powers impinge upon his own, for good or ill. These are the gods.

The gods may be born out of single vivid impressions. The cult of such "momentary gods" (as they have been termed) seems to go back to very early times, although into the period of their highly literate culture the Greeks retained the notion of the "momentary god" or *daimon* belonging to separate activities or experiences. These were abstract as well as concrete: they deified Chance as well as Wine, Reason as well as Wealth. Socrates attributed his skill in philosophic discourse to his obeying his personal *daimon*. Then, many early deities are "functional gods" closely bound to the economic activity of the tribe. Anthropologists tell us that the people who serve functional gods and look to them to supply the harvest, or the fertility of herds, do not differentiate between the work which they do (tilling the ground, etc.) and the ritual believed to ensure the god's continued favor and activity. Everything falls under the religious duty of the worshipper, who must acknowledge the nature of his god, and behave accordingly so that the god will do his part. Later sophistication recognizes the diversity of the world by grouping the gods into a pantheon, where each god has a part to play in relation to all the rest. Here the more important gods take over the functions of several earlier gods, including their names. We can see this process in the deities of Mount Olympus, where the Immortals represent collectively the whole gamut of Greek life organized under the rule of a supreme god Zeus, the All-Father. War, sexual love, marriage, city-organization and law, corn-growing, grape-growing, the artisan's work, and so on, appear as Ares, Aphrodite, Hera, Athene, Demeter, Dionysus, Hephaestus, and the rest.

The gods, as immortal collectively (although individually they may die and be replaced by other gods), represent the continuity of life through the generations of men. The divine world known to mythic thinking pictures man's longing for permanence in the midst of change, and his conviction that life is stronger than death.

Mircea Eliade has tried to find a central logic that underlies all the bewildering diversity of myth. He argues that this emerges in the constant appearance of two categories that myth calls into being, namely, sacred time

49

and sacred space.[3] Sacred time is meaningful time in contrast to profane time, which is "dead" time, or time which
destroys man's being by making him the prey of decay and
death. Mythic thinking envisages a resurrection out of
"dead" time by what Eliade terms "a return to the beginnings" or a recovery of "primal time." Myth posits the existence of an original wholeness and perfection that has been
lost, leaving man ensnared in the present imperfect state
where all his efforts seem to lead him further away from
the ideal existence of which he dreams. But myth, which
holds the word that alone links him to primal time, can
make what has been lost live once more in the present.
Through the retelling of the myth, and through the enact-
ment of ritual embodying the word of the myth, that
which has been swallowed up by time is disgorged by
time. Once more the beginnings that were before time
began its deadly work are present. Sacred time, then, is
the presentness of eternity, the blessedness of knowledge
that secular time denies and thinks impossible. Man, so
long as he holds to sacred time, lives with the divine and
himself achieves divinity.

Sacred space is of the same order, and is achieved by
the same means: myth and ritual. The centralization of
religious rites in one sanctuary or holy place, which is
then frequently called the center, or the "navel of the
world," is an illustration of the end that is sought whenever
any space is marked out as sacred. Such a space does not
so much signify that the divine is localized somewhere on
earth as that profane space is prohibited from extending
indefinitely. Where the profane ends there sacred space
establishes itself. (The word "profane," we may remember,
means "in front of the fane or temple.") Just as sacred time
banishes "dead," meaningless time, so sacred space banishes "empty," meaningless space. Dead time crushes and
kills the living spirit by its weight, pressing man down under
upon his grave. (Even today, we sometimes speak jocularly
of time as "the Enemy.") Sacred time frees man and gives
him eternal life. Empty space, equally, makes for man an

[3] *The Sacred and the Profane: The Nature of Religion* is, perhaps,
the basic work out of many in which Eliade sets out his views on
myth and religion.

immovable center, creates an orderly universe. There man is always at home, knowing a bliss from which nothing on earth can remove him. He dwells among the gods.

Mythic language is complex, and I have been able here to touch on only a few aspects of it. Yet perhaps enough has been said for us to go on and ask how we are to regard it. If myth makes the gods and brings into existence all the religions of mankind, is it a sufficient explanation of every faith man has known, whether that faith is "primitive" or "advanced"? Is myth an ultimate category? Must we simply choose between accepting myth or rejecting it? Such questions deserve an answer.

In the preceding lecture I considered the empirical and the idealistic approaches to language. I shall now take up these same two approaches to myth, and then follow with my own answer in terms that I call (without justifying the label at present) the historical.

Three Answers to the Question of Myth

(A) THE EMPIRICAL ANSWER

The empirical view of myth is that it exists in order to be overcome. However important it may have been in permitting primitive man to organize his world, the fact that it no longer rules our thinking speaks for itself. It is prelogical thinking, and it has proved its inadequacy by making itself obsolete. It has given way to logical thinking, and finally to scientific thinking. Man no longer seeks to console himself for his failure to cope with his present environment by seeking to recover a mythical golden age in the past. Now he knows that the world he lives in may be made a fit place to live in by the use of his intelligence. No longer need he seek to placate powers beyond himself, for he is able to recognize the true nature of those powers and control them, not by ritual and incantation, but through the technology that the patient investigation of nature makes possible. Mythology belongs to the "disease" of speech, the laws of which are now investigated through linguistic analysis and applied through information theory.

One place where empiricism may find myth of more

than historical interest is in the study of the human psyche. Already in the nineteenth century Auguste Comte formulated his celebrated theory of the three stages of human thought: the religious, the metaphysical, and the positive (or scientific). Although Comte believed that man had arrived at the third stage, he recognized that our *imaginations* carry over primitive habits. He therefore devised a new "religion of humanity" that should take care of these final vestiges of the religious attitude to the world. The content of this new religion was adapted to present knowledge, and nonsupernatural, but the forms it used were drawn from traditional Catholic liturgy. Comte thought this should be enough to appease the old ghosts not yet laid to rest in the internal consciousness. Modern psychoanalysis had been responsible for a revival of Comte's basic premise here, though with refinements stemming from knowledge of the unconscious mind.

Sigmund Freud thought of religion as an illusion destined to fade away before the all-conquering scientific attitude to existence. Nevertheless, some neo-Freudians have revised his negative judgment on religion, while retaining his basic assumptions. Eliade has observed that the Freudian technique of depth-analysis is oddly parallel to the mythic reading of the world. Where religious ritual seeks to reinstate a lost "primal time" before man's fall from innocence, so analysis seeks to take the patient back to early childhood, before some traumatic experience broke into his psychic life and left it with a load of guilt that has induced neurosis. Although the conscious mind may think logically, the unconscious mind retains archaic modes of interpreting the world and apprehends existence mythically.[4] Freud admitted the usefulness of religious belief in earlier times, since it helped the individual adjust himself to the demands of nature and society. Men were prepared to accept, as the will of the gods, the necessary restrictions and pains of life. Rabbi Richard Rubenstein, on general Freudian lines, has argued that religious doctrines generally, though they correspond to nothing objective in the outside world, nevertheless make very good sense of the

---

[4] See *Myth and Reality*, pp. 76-79.

interior world.[5] He believes that religion still has not merely a valuable but an essential role to play in allowing
modern man to live in society and (as he phrases it) "to
have good dreams." For this purpose — although literal
belief in religious dogmas is impossible — religious liturgy
alone speaks the word that allows the psyche to accept
the repressions that social life imposes upon it. In particular, such psychically vulnerable experiences as puberty,
marriage, parenthood, and bereavement all require support from the "meaning" that religion gives to them. Moreover, because the healing word comes through traditional
religious myths current in the individual's religious inher-
itance, no artificially constructed religion will do. Only
that faith to which a man is born heir because of his
existential circumstances can furnish the myths that can
support his preconscious needs and undergird his personal
experience.

To sum up: the empirical answer to the question of the
significance of myth cannot go further than to say that
myth may perhaps satisfy the subjective demands of the
insecure self. Of no objective import, myths are a storehouse of images of the world that men inhabit insofar as
they are heirs of a prescientific past. Religious images and
the logic of the myths that unite those images linger on,
even though the world they present is no longer believable.
The mythic world was the construction of the childhood
of the human race. It persists today simply in the imagination of the child that every modern man, even in maturity,
carries within him. In spite of the fact that man today
has "come of age," the interior child still understands
nothing beyond the language of humanity's childhood, the
language of myth. And so that child has to be appeased
in order to keep him quiet.

(B) THE IDEALISTIC ANSWER

The idealistic answer to the significance of myth begins
by pointing out some human facts ignored by the empiricist.

First, the growth of scientific knowledge has alienated
man from his environment. Although we have gained tech-

---

[5] See his *After Auschwitz: Radical Theology and Contemporary Judaism.*

nological mastery over things, we seem unable to live happily with them. The words of Jesus are confirmed: it profits little for man to gain the whole world and lose his soul. Second, today there are unprecedented means of communication available to us; and yet we are conscious of a serious breakdown in communication. There is an overproduction of words, and a famine of meaning. Third, the promises of rationalism and scientism have been proved false. Man's freedom was to be the reward of getting rid of bondage to religious superstition. Yet, with the disappearance of transcendent goals, daily existence has become increasingly burdensome — a rat-race in a mechanized and computerized cage. Even if we journey to the moon, we simply exchange the mud of earth for moondust. We extend our prison walls but cannot step outside them. We are at once trapped captives and homeless wanderers over the surface of life. Religious consciousness alone can make us free men by restoring to life what Paul Tillich has called its "depth dimension." Recognizing our ability to transcend the phenomenal world in our ability to use mythic language, we recover our human birthright to move in eternity as well as in time.

As much as empiricism, nevertheless, idealism insists on the primitive origins of mythological thinking. Myths now have to be interpreted from the standpoint of a sophisticated intelligence that is fully aware that no individual myth can be literally true. What divides the two standpoints is a diverse understanding of that "real world" which mythic language presents in symbolic terms. For the empiricist the real world is the objective sum of things separated from subjective distortions. Hence, all language disguises true thought, because it has not yet freed itself from mythic language, which is mankind's first fumbling efforts towards thinking. For the idealist the real world is the world of Being beyond existence in space and time, that is, beyond the split of reality into subjects and objects. Mythic language is, therefore, essential language that "remembers" an original wholeness that has been lost. It is not merely a primitive mode of language to be outgrown. However, when used by primitive peoples, myth falsely objectivizes the reality it intuits. Primitive belief projects

54

the symbols of mythic language into space and time as though they were objects actually existing there. It treats myths as though they were literal descriptions of the working of nature (or of *super-nature,* a realm conceived to exist somehow parallel to nature, and peopled by heavenly beings as nature is peopled by earthly beings).

The idealist believes that all language that has not degenerated into mere denotative signs is language that simultaneously conceals and reveals thought. Mythic language conceals thought insofar as it seems to point to the so-called objective world of phenomena. It reveals thought insofar as it conveys reality or transphenomenal Being to the thinking subject. Therefore, the idealist *demythologizes* myth. He takes it out of childish use and makes it available in the service of mature thought. He removes from each myth under consideration any reference to the empirical or "objective" world, retaining solely its use as a symbol of transphenomenal reality. He does so in order to strip away the "concealing" aspect of mythic language, allowing its "revealing" aspect to stand forth as self-justifying truth.

For example, suppose the idealist looks at the myth of Zeus. The myth talks about a father of the gods, dwelling upon Mount Olympus and directing the affairs of gods and men. The childish imagination sees a magnified man, unscrupulous and devious, but one to be feared and obeyed because of his unlimited power, which can cast thunderbolts at rebels. The idealist explains that Zeus was always "really" the religious symbol of the power of Being (experienced in both its constructive and destructive aspects). But, since symbols are born and die within the human consciousness, this particular symbol is a dead one. Once Zeus was a symbol to mediate Being. Now that particular symbol has merely historical interest, and lives in the memory of Western culture alone.

If we turn to the symbol Jesus Christ, however, we encounter a symbol that still lives. Jesus, unlike Zeus, was an actual individual in history. Yet he would not have become a focus for worship had he not become identified with the religious symbol of the Christ. He does not live as a symbol because of his individual life (without which,

55

in any case, we know very little) but because there are still subjects who regard him as *the* symbol of the power of Being immanent in human life.[6]

In this fashion the idealist would argue. And, so he would continue, by identifying the original symbol of Jewish faith, the Messiah, with the subsequent symbol of the Son of God (explained in Christian doctrine as unity of substance with God the Father), Christians have kept this symbol alive and meaningful. Its meaning, however, depends upon a continued experience within living subjects of the power of this particular symbol to mediate to them what the symbol signifies. The myth of a supernatural man from heaven is no longer believable. It was believable in New Testament times, and it continued to be believable for a long time. Dante, for example, was able to describe the geography of hell, purgatory, and heaven in terms of the then-current cosmological beliefs. But once exploration had proved that the other side of the world was not inaccessible and that hell was not located under the earth, belief in the heavenly-man myth was no longer rational. Finally the Copernican cosmology abolished the concept of a highest heaven or empyrean that could serve as the dwelling-place of God. Once this cosmology had fully taken hold of the imagination of Western man, the symbol

---

[6] Basic to the idealistic position is the belief that the individual has true being and meaning solely to the extent to which he reflects (symbolizes) a universal essence. Thus Philip Wheelwright writes: "The Christian doctrine that every individual man falls from grace through Adam's sin and receives new life through Christ's death and resurrection exemplifies the sense of effective concrete universality on a higher level. The doctrine becomes intelligible when Adam, and when Christ, are understood not as atomistically distinct beings but as truly participating in the essence of all mankind and as epitomizing that essence in themselves" (*The Burning Fountain*, p. 152). Although he is at pains to combat the "positivistic" limitation of language, Wheelwright does not explicitly develop an idealistic epistemology. Yet it is significant that he employs Hegel's category of the concrete universal. And the title of his book, *The Burning Fountain*, is derived from the Platonic statement of the identity of the human spirit with the Eternal expressed in Shelley's *Adonais*:

> Dust to dust; but the pure spirit shall flow
> Back to the burning fountain whence it came,
> A portion of the Eternal, which must glow
> Through time and change, unquenchably the same.

was dead. The persistence of the myth, if it is insisted on as a fact instead of as a "meaningful" symbol, creates an obstacle preventing contemporary man from seeing his life empowered by Being. It fails to mediate to him the reality of the eternal in the temporal that prevents his being from being overwhelmed by the transience of existence in time and space. Yet, *some* myth is essential for human wholeness. Man deprived of myth is deprived of both a "self" and a "world."

(c) THE HISTORICAL ANSWER

The historical answer to the significance of myth, as I shall speak of it, cannot simply be identified with the viewpoint of historians. Individual historians frequently incline either to an empirical or to an idealistic estimate of historical phenomena. In choosing the word *historical* as a label to contrast with both *empirical* and *idealistic*, I wish to indicate first of all (and in a general, "common sense" fashion) a viewpoint that recognizes concrete existence in space and time as real. And, in particular, I have in mind that attitude to existence which we find in Judaism and Christianity, and which has earned for these the title of *historical religions*. It is in the Scriptures of the Old and the New Testaments, I believe, that we find a genuine alternative to the two interpretations of myth already reviewed.

The historical approach to the world has some features in common with the empirical approach. It has no hesitation, for example, in describing myths of the gods as false. In the Old Testament the religious cults of the Gentiles are strenuously denounced on the basis that the gods they honor do not exist. In the New Testament the worship of the pagan ,deities is ascribed to their worshippers' living in "times of ignorance" (Acts 17:30; I Pet. 1:14). It is of interest, too, that the word *mythos* in the New Testament always means simply a fable or fanciful story. There is no thought of mythic language conveying a higher truth than can be found in the "profane" world — quite the reverse. Isaiah leaves us in no doubt that the idol-maker is self-deceived when he imagines his material to be more than a simple piece of wood (Isa. 44:19). Paul and Barnabas at Lystra, confronted by pagan beliefs, exhort the people to turn from such follies (Acts 14:15). Thus, the historical outlook shares with the empirical the conviction that there is a real world of objects presented to our senses which has its own validity apart from the subject's estimate of it. Our awareness does not make the world, but rather our mind must adapt itself to what is there to be known.

On the other hand, the historical view does not place restrictions on what this real world can contain. Because of the biblical indifference to "religion" as a general category and its determined hostility toward the religious assumptions of the nations outside the covenant, some theologians have followed Friedrich Gogarten's thesis that the Bible contains a logic that drives towards a wholly secular understanding of the universe. This is a completely impossible position to defend from a Christian stance, since both the Old and the New Testaments attack only idolatry and false beliefs leaving men "without God in the world" (Eph. 2:12), and demand the establishment of a holy people united in the worship of the God who made heaven and earth. In approaching pagan audiences, Paul was ready to admit that pagan worship contained at least a remnant of the acknowledgment of the divine Creator that every creature ought to make because he could not be wholly without a sense of God's goodness (Acts 17). On the historical view, leaving behind belief in myths and abandoning all distinction between the sacred and the secular are two very different things. The real world comes into clearer focus as we abandon superstitious notions about it. Yet "true religion" belongs to this real world, and recognition of the suprasensible reality of the one true God is essential to an existence seeing things as they really are.

At this point an objection might be raised. Some would argue that the historical viewpoint is an incoherent compromise between the empirical and the idealistic world pictures. To deny myth is to deny religion. It is to recognize every case of bringing the divine in to "explain" the character of objective reality as a primitive construct. On the other hand, to retain belief in a "God" who exists in a "heaven" inaccessible to sense experience and who requires worship because human existence finds its meaning and purpose in obeying His "will" — this is to demand from man a self-understanding that makes sense only on the supposition that mythic language is man's passport to transphenomenal reality. The God of the Judeo-Christian religion is no more true and no more false than the gods of every other religion. He may be, of course, a more adequate symbol of the real world that lies behind phenomena. Picturing our existence in the terms provided in the biblical religious tradition may be a more complete unveiling of the truth, a more decisive revelation of Being, than any other religious language can convey. But, in any case, the religious message about this God comes to us from the myth-believing past clothed in mythical dress. Equally with every other religious message, the biblical message today reveals its meaning properly only after it has been demythologized. A literal God in a literal heaven commanding us to accept objectified information about our existence in time and space is a relic of an archaic stage in man's evolving consciousness. To believe in such a God is to close our eyes to the whole development of world religions. It is to speak in a language that has ceased to have any meaning today.

The answer to both these objections is contained in the argument with which I closed my first lecture, namely, that empiricism and idealism alike fail to take existence seriously enough. Empiricism, seeking the objective world, forgets that the objective stands forth only as it is known in subjects. Idealism, seeking to transcend the cleavage between subject and object in order to grasp their primal unity, surrenders the reality of the object and listens only to the testimony of the subject.[7]

Thus, empiricism judges myth to be descriptive solely of the inner, subjective consciousness. It can have no objective reference whatsoever. Therefore, all religious statements (being the product of mythic thinking) are literally nonsensical, however meaningful they may be subjectively. Idealism finds the literal absurdity of myth to be proof

---

[7] The whole question touched on here is discussed in James Brown's book *Subject and Object in Modern Theology.*

that the facticity of phenomena is expendable. Things are simply *what they mean* for the thinking subject; they have no independent existence in themselves. Against the first position, the historical approach to existence protests that objective reality need not be limited *a priori* to what may be reported by subjects looking outward to empirically observable objects and using descriptive, notational language. Language formed on the basis of myth may well be able to convey real information that cannot be communicated in other terms. Religious language, then, may be the necessary and proper medium for speaking the truth about the religious object, God, who is known only by existing subjects. On this basis, religious statements will not be all on one level. They will be true or false according to whether or not they truly represent their object. Whether or not they happen to be true will depend, not upon the nature of the language used, but upon their reality-content. Because some religious statements are false does not mean that all are. Indeed, the meaningfulness of religious statements in general demands the recognition that to affirm some must be to reject others.

Here it becomes clear that to avoid the Scylla of empiricism, we must also steer clear of the Charybdis of idealism. Asserting that religious language can refer to objective reality means asserting also that religious language cannot consist essentially of myths requiring to be demythologized in order to uncover their "real," nonobjectified meaning. Yet, since religion and myth manifestly go together, how can we escape the conclusion that denial of the literal truth of myth leads us either to jettison *all* religious language or else to concur in the conclusion that the truth of religion is nonobjective?

We can escape from this dilemma, I believe, by taking into consideration the rootage of myth in actual, historical existence.

Mythic Language: "Feeling After" God

Myth, I suggested earlier, is story. And stories arise out of our concrete experience of living as conscious subjects who find meaning in the events through which we live. In our daily existence we become aware of patterns linking discrete experiences into a meaningful whole. We find it possible to *tell the story* of what has happened to us through patterns of (teleologically) significant items lifted out of the flux of time. "One crowded hour of glorious life / Is worth an age without a name." Certainly! Because *homo loquens* gives a "name" to that hour by telling its story, and lets the rest slip back into oblivion. The story gives us victory over "dead" time.

Myth, however, is not story as such, but always the story of the gods. Those powers in man's experience that are not his to command are crucially important, for they give his personal story its essential context. Thus the gods, by limiting man and thwarting his will until he learns to cooperate with them, help man to know who he is and what his place is in the world. These gods are the "immortals," whose stories are told in myths that are eternal — in the sense that they are not restricted to any human time and never lose their truth. These gods provide the cosmic patterns by which the patterns of human existence are understood.[8]

Now, insofar as the primitive gods are linked with external nature, they tend to lose their divinity after they have been named in human language, and thus brought under human power. Man would never come to know the world of calendar time and the seasons unless he had first told himself the stories of the struggle between the gods of light and darkness, and why the seasonal gods rule in turn over the months marked by the moon goddess who continually uncovers, and veils again, her shining face. But, afterwards, he knows the patterns will remain constant and dependable. Here Comte's theory of the three stages leading to "positive" (i.e. scientific) knowledge has plausibility.

In the history of language, we can see the dismissal of the gods who have served their purpose through the detachment of poetry from religion. Poetic language continues the work of myth by illuminating human experience

---

[8] "Because myth relates the *gesta* of Supernatural Beings and the manifestations of their sacred powers, it becomes the exemplary model for all significant human activities"; Eliade, *Myth and Reality*, p. 6.

through making new patterns, and thus opening fresh aspects of the world that enlarge its meaning. Heidegger describes the poet as the priest of mankind, the one who names the gods and speaks forth the world of meaning that Being addresses to him. The description is not inept, if we discount its idealistic slant. Wordsworth said the same thing more directly (and I think more accurately) when he spoke of "nature's priest." But the difference between poetry and myth is that the poet is no longer literally a priest. The "gods" he names are not worshipped. Art has been sundered from religion. For the Greeks the poet was still recognized as a maker (*poietes*, from *poiein*, "to make") and his work was supposed to be inspired by a god. Today the word "inspiration" applied to artistic creation is recognized to be wholly a figure of speech.

Then, if myth turns into poetry, is religion destined to wither away except as a storehouse of poetic symbols? I would personally answer Yes — unless there are stories of the gods that are real and historical in the sense of having actual relation to existence. And such is the claim of the Judeo-Christian religion, which is fully prepared to say that all the gods are *merely* mythical, but the one true God has revealed Himself in human history. I would add that the dismissal of myth in the historical view is to be distinguished from *demythologizing*, which is an inadequate way of dealing with myth because it fails to see myth in the light of history and to measure it against the full reality of existence.

The empirical way of demythologizing is to say that myth is false as a description of objective, external reality, but true as a description of the inner, subjective life of man. The idealistic way is to say that myth is false when objectified, and true when read as symbolic language revealing transphenomenal reality. The historical view is that myth is not, and never was true. But it has an historical explanation. It was a distorted response to the reality of God — man's Creator — created in the situation of man's sinful refusal to know and honor the one true God. The gods of myth are not purely a primitive description of the forces of nature, but also a "feeling after God" (Acts 17:27).

This cannot mean, of course, that myth is merely super-stition and serves no purpose at all. Historical faith be-lieves that God's goodness is never deflected by human sinfulness, but that He brings good out of evil. Humanly speaking, man's ability to speak about God comes from his having learned to name the gods. The true religion is born in the midst of the many false religions. When the patterns of myth are seen to be what they are, namely, patterns of human speaking concerning historical exis-tence,[9] all the richness of language becomes available for speaking about God and thus learning to know Him with our minds. For God does not reveal Himself to us, and He does not speak to us, except as human beings living con-cretely in an historical context. The Scriptures did not fall down from heaven, as the Koran is supposed to have done. The Word of God comes to us as the words of men, men rooted in their times and speaking the language of their country. And the Word become flesh, who did not despise the virgin's womb, did not despise either the language and the cultural patterns of a first-century Jew living within the Romano-Hellenistic world.

How human language, formed on patterns that have grown out of myth, can convey to us the truth of God's own revelation: this is the subject of my next two lectures.

---

[9] Eliade draws attention to the fact that, in societies where myths are still essential to the interpretation of life as part of an unques-tioned way of knowledge, a distinction is always made between "true stories" and "false stories." The former are stories concerning the gods and supernatural beings, while the latter are stories of heroes or miraculous animals. The first alone — the genuine myths — *concern them directly,* in that they explain the human condition as such, while the latter merely explain changes in the external world. Archaic man, says Eliade, thus sets an unconditional value upon myths. "Myth teaches him the primordial 'stories' that have consti-tuted him existentially; and everything connected with his existence and his legitimate mode of existence in the Cosmos concerns him directly" (*Myth and Reality,* p. 12).

Chapter 3

The Authority of the Divine Word

I BEGAN BY PROMISING TO LOOK AT THE THEOLOGICAL perspective on language. Yet only toward the end of the second lecture did I actually mention the positive relation of language to the Christian gospel — although this was supposed to be my chief concern. One may rightly object that I have been very slow in coming to the point: my response is that finding the point may perhaps be most of the problem.

By investigating two contrasting philosophical approaches to language, neither of which finds room for the message of historic Christianity, I have sought to find why it is that these are both inadequate theologically. In my first lecture I suggested that both fail to do justice to the full dimension of existence. (Or, to put the matter in another way, both make restrictive metaphysical assumptions.) Empiricism, approaching language via the object that language describes, assumes that either language describes sense-experience or else misleads us into believing in nonexistent entities. Idealism, approaching language via the subject who uses language to discover meaning, assumes that all meaning arises out of the subject's participation in transphenomenal reality; and that the subject is made aware of this participation through the power of language within him. The former viewpoint tends to deny that the subject can do anything meaningful with words except use them to construct a language of signs (Hobbes' "counters"), one allowing the objective

65

world to declare itself clearly and unambiguously. Even when it is prepared to admit the possibility of different uses of language, it still finds meaning located in the observable world. The latter viewpoint denies that the objective world has any meaning for the subject, except insofar as sensory experience provides verbal material from which the subject draws in order to discover his "world" (Bultmann's "demythologized myth"), a world of pure consciousness breaking through the limits of time and space.

Thus, between the two, we are asked to choose either actuality without God, or God without actuality. We can have creation at the price of not being able to speak of its Creator, or we can have a God who does not create and who is known only in a world negating existence with its distinction between subject and object.

In my second lecture I suggested that mythic language raises the question of history. Once again, empiricism and idealism give us a choice making Christian theology impossible. With the empiricists, we may choose the reading of history that judges myth to have been a dead-end road on mankind's journey from ignorance to knowledge, a naively subjective method of looking at the world now withering away (except in the uneducable subconscious mind). Therefore religion, being the product of myth, is destined to disappear from history. Or, with the idealists, we may accept a reading of history that takes myth to be the basic form of genuinely human speech. Therefore, religion mediated through myth is as deathless as humanity itself. Nevertheless, the various religions of mankind must suffer a sea-change, following the change in consciousness of modern man. Their specific teachings are no longer believable, taken literally. Today we know that myth does not describe the phenomenal world, but instead symbolizes the transcendent world of meaning.

Taking the empirical view, we must then say that revelation is impossible. There are simply words stating empirically verifiable propositional truths (Wittgenstein's "what the case is") and words exhorting us to behave in humanly profitable ways. Taking the idealistic view, we must say that all meaningful speech is revelatory. Our words are without final significance unless they reflect the eternal voiceless Word that lies behind all words.

Christian faith, however, is able to read history in a manner that is more flexible and more inclusive than either empiricism or idealism. It does not deny that history exhibits an advance in human consciousness that is mirrored in the growth of language. It gladly admits that better knowledge of the objective world has made religions founded upon a literal acceptance of myth untenable. It grants, equally gladly, that man cannot express human meaning without making use of symbolic language; and, to this extent, he remains a mythmaking creature. However, it contends that the material of religious faith is by no means identical with myth, either literally believed or taken symbolically. For, historically, myth can be seen to have developed into poetic speech, or language structured by the symbol or word-image. And the Christian religion is not simply poetry.[1] Christianity puts forward propositions concerning the objective world, propositions that do not yield empirically verifiable information about objects. The propositions of Christianity relate primarily to subjects: God and ourselves. The Christian believes that his faith, while giving him no privileged instruction about "what the case is" in the created world, nevertheless gives him essential knowledge about the world, as divinely created. It also gives him assurance of the human meaning of his existence. It mediates this meaning beyond the reaches of

---

[1] In the eyes of the idealist, poetry does indeed carry a religious value. As the purest and least earthbound kind of speech, it opens our consciousness to the transcendent world. The Romantic poets, who were influenced by (and themselves influenced) idealistic philosophers, sometimes made claims to a religious status for their art. Samuel Taylor Coleridge, for example, believed the poetic imagination to be a direct reflection of the Primary Imagination that was "a repetition in the finite mind of the eternal act of creation in the infinite I Am." Many nineteenth-century thinkers — Matthew Arnold among them — held that the inner truth of all religions was in being poetic truth. And for others (Walter Pater, e.g.) aesthetic experience was the heir of religious experience, the only form of transcendence believable in the modern world. The aesthetic creed asserting that art — or, more widely, "culture" — is the real religion of modernity has still wide currency today.

67

his own consciousness and beyond the "world" that human consciousness as such creates for itself.

Christian faith asserts that there is a divine revelation that has been given in history and that involves the objective, spatio-temporal universe where the Creator has made Himself known to His creation. It asserts that the divine revelation comes, not to the universal symbol-making-and-interpreting human consciousness that is essentially eternal, but to individual men in their actual, concrete existences. And it asserts that the source of God's self-disclosure cannot be found within human nature as such. It is not the reverberation in man of a divine element attuned to the eternal Logos. It is the objective Word of God Himself addressing men with His own authority, through the power of His Holy Spirit.

The Word of God in the Old and New Testaments is never a symbolic word merely, but always an actual communication. It appears as an actual statement or command addressed to particular people at a particular time, and with a content that is to be understood quite objectively. Scripture is nothing if not specific. The biblical words carry a concrete content: "Hear, O Israel: The Lord our God is one Lord" (Deut. 6:4); and, "This is my beloved Son, in whom I am well pleased; hear ye him" (Matt. 17:5).

"Imaging" the Divine

The authority of the divine Word for Christian faith *is* final for Christian believers. That is, there is no possibility of going "behind" or "beyond" this Word in order to establish its right to command allegiance and belief. Yet the Word is not arbitrary and inexplicable, in the sense that it commands assent for no possible reason except that it is a command. Indeed, the Word is not an "it" — an inscrutable force or faceless categorical imperative — at all. The Word is God revealing Himself. And the Word comes as promise as well as command; as Light, and Truth, and Love as well as mystery and inconceivable power.

In this respect the Word of Christian revelation is very different from the "Word" that idealism assumes to give Being to words. As we have seen, the "Word" of idealism is likened by Heidegger to walking away from the habitations of men into the darkness. A similar thought was expressed, less poetically, by Karl Jaspers in an exchange that he carried on some years ago with Bultmann. Jaspers objected that Bultmann's program of demythologizing did not sufficiently delineate the real function of myth, or, at any rate, did not place it in proper perspective. Jaspers writes:

> The real task, therefore, is not to demythologize, but to recover mythical thought in its original purity, and to appropriate, in this form of thinking, the marvelous mythical contents that deepen us morally, enlarge us as human beings, and indirectly bring us closer to the lofty, imageless transcendence, the idea of God which no myth can fully express for it surpasses them all.[2]

Here Jaspers takes for granted that the essence of God, His "idea," is *imageless transcendence*. This assumption is a constant one in idealistic thinking, and underlies the whole rationale for taking mythic thinking to be the way of uncovering the wordless "Word" giving meaning to human words. Because the idealistic divine "Word" is imageless, symbols can only *indirectly bring us closer* — never actually reach — its transcendent ineffability. Quite in line with Jaspers, Heidegger in his "Conversation on a Country Path About Thinking" draws his dialogue to an end by commenting on the single word constituting Fragment 122 of Heraclitus: *anchibasie* or "going towards." Mortals can *go towards* Being, but the journey is a never-ending one, for ultimate reality is always out of reach of finite intelligence.[3] So too Paul Tillich modified in the second volume of his *Systematic Theology* the statement he made in the first volume, where he called Being-itself the sole nonsymbolic statement we can make about God. In his revised statement, Tillich says that even to call God Being-itself is to speak at once symbolically and nonsymbolically.

---

[2] *Myth and Christianity*, p. 17. Note that Jaspers is not contradicting Bultmann so much as trying to follow through to its proper conclusion that which, so Jaspers thinks, Bultmann's own starting-point assumes but which his "orthodoxy" prevents him from affirming.

[3] *Discourse on Thinking*, pp. 88-89. The "Teacher" in the conversation, representing Heidegger himself, says that he prefers to translate this word of Heraclitus by "moving-into-nearness."

So he concludes that there comes a point "at which we must speak non-symbolically about God, but in terms of a quest for Him."

That God, the Infinite Spirit, is unknowable in Himself is an affirmation made by Christian theology throughout its history. But that our approach to Him is one of "going towards" or of engaging on "a quest" for Him is utterly alien to the whole perspective of Christian faith. For the biblical foundation on which Christian theology is built states with unmistakable clarity that, though we can never approach nearer to Him by our own volition or through our own wisdom, He has come to us. God's revelation of Himself is complete and final, not tentative or partial. God spoke by the prophets and has spoken finally by His Son (Heb. 1:1-2).

Certainly it is the utter transcendence of God — His distance from His creation as the Creator — that makes it impossible for us to find images by which we can (paraphrasing Heidegger) "near His distance in the heavens." This is the reason for the scriptural prohibition against making images of God. God is indeed the sole sovereign, "who only hath immortality, dwelling in the light which no man can approach unto; whom no man hath seen, nor can see" (I Tim. 6:16). But this is the same God who makes Himself near to those to whom He wills to reveal Himself. This is the God of whom Isaiah could speak, saying, "I saw also the Lord sitting upon a throne, high and lifted up" (Isa. 6:1). God in the Bible is as unlike "imageless transcendence" as it is possible to be. The abundance of rich verbal images used to describe God — from Genesis through to Revelation — gives the lie to such a concept. And although it may be agreed that all verbal images in Scripture present no more than *aspects* of God in relation to His people, in the New Testament Jesus Christ is declared to be "the express image of his person" (Heb. 1:3). All partial words about God are completed in the revelation of the Word made flesh.

At this point I should like to stress that the concept of God as imageless transcendence, far from placing any check upon idolatry, is precisely the reflection of the inner logic of idolatry. When an idol is made and placed within a temple, the motive for the action is to be explained in terms of the mythic consciousness. The idol itself represents those *mythical contents* that, according to Jaspers, deepen us morally, enlarge us as human beings, and indirectly bring us closer to the imageless divine. By its presence within the holy place, the idol ensures that the worshipper shall know the place *really* to be holy — sacred space marked out clearly in separation from profane space. The idol-worshipper worships, of course, not the actual material of the image, but the power of divinity that it images — the same power he learns through myths telling of the activities of this god. Essentially, the idol serves as a symbol for the godhead of the god, rather than as the god himself. Even the sanctity of the image itself derives chiefly from the numinous aura that the god causes to surround this focus of sacred space, making the image inseparable from that which it images.

In historical fact, culturally minded defenders of image worship in classical times made this point the basis of their argument.[4] They pointed out that only ignorant and superstitious persons ever came near to identifying the image with the god. The enlightened, however, revered the image wholly for what it represented, namely, the spiritual reality given "a local habitation and a name" in order that men should not forget to be pious, but should have before their eyes a reminder that they served a reality surpassing all the worship that any individual god could demand. Wrote Epictetus: "If an image of your God was in the room, you would not behave as you do, and yet when God is within you and oversees and overhears everything, you are not ashamed to think and act in this way."

The words of Epictetus indicate that image worship leads, when sophistication supplants primitive world-views, to belief in the imageless transcendence of the *god within,* the Word that speaks of the eternal in the temporal giving self-understanding. There is a direct line between religion founded in myth and the so-called "purity" of the religious imagination that deepens us morally and enlarges

---

[4] See Edwyn Bevan, *Holy Images: An Inquiry into Idolatry and Image Worship in Ancient Paganism and in Christianity,* especially Lecture 2.

us as human beings (Jaspers). Central to this whole way of viewing reality is the belief that the authority of revelation lies within our own self-consciousness. The symbol, originally created out of the raw materials of mythic language, exists in order to be demythologized, and therefore to allow its phenomenal aspect as a determinate actuality to fade in the light of the imageless transcendent, the transphenomenal reality that lives in our subjectivity beyond the limiting bounds of our individual history.

The biblical proscription of idolatry, then, cannot be limited to the one historical situation in which idol worship was the common form of ethnic worship. (One is reminded, here, of the agnostic who was asked by a seriously minded believer whether he was able to keep the Ten Commandments. He replied, "Well, I've never really wanted to make a graven image!") When the First Epistle of John ends with the admonition, "Little children, keep yourselves from idols" (I John 5:21), we cannot think that the writer is thinking primarily of his hearers lapsing into crude paganism. He has been speaking of the false teaching that has crept into the church, particularly the Gnostic denial that Jesus Christ has come in the flesh.[5] For the Christian, idolatry is mythic thinking at one level or another whether primitive or sophisticated. Idolatry, after all, is always a spiritual attitude. (It is certainly not a materialist one, for the materialist is tempted neither to make graven images nor to "near" himself to imageless

[5] This interpretation has not been universally accepted, largely because elsewhere in the New Testament *eidola* stand for literal images. The large number of pagan temples and shrines at Ephesus has been cited as the reason for the warning here. Yet the letter contains otherwise no reference to pagan worship, and expositors as early as Westcott (1883) refer to the likelihood that the intention was to underline the dominant argument against false teaching on Gnostic lines within the Christian community. In his *Open Letter to Evangelicals: A Devotional and Homiletic Commentary on the First Epistle of John*, R. E. O. White gives a careful examination of previous views. He concludes: "An exposition of tests for distinguishing true from false, genuine from counterfeit, fittingly ends with an appeal to beware *shams:* but as the shams in question are religious, and as the intellectual pretensions of the Gnostics made them contemptuous of the common people's love of idolatry, it was especially appropriate, and forceful, to choose for 'shams' the loaded word 'idols'" (p. 267).

transcendence.) Against idolatry in any and every form, biblical faith asserts that the one true God has made Himself known in history. In order to hear the divine Word, we do not have to manufacture images in which we can catch the echoes that can sound within our spiritual ears alone. God speaks through His Holy Spirit in words that are, in their origin, ordinary, earthly, historically fashioned words. He reveals Himself in such a fashion that earthly images are not incapable of truly representing His transcendent existence and His Holy Will. Human words and human thoughts cannot "contain" God; but, when God wills it, they become authentic means of our knowing Him.[6]

[6] It has been argued frequently that Barth and Bultmann begin from a common base in that both reject the possibility of God's being the object of man's thought. (Barth in the second edition of his *Romans* said that he kept continually in mind Kierkegaard's dictum concerning the absolute qualitative distinction between time and eternity.) But, in fact, the divergence between the two theologians appears precisely in the way in which God's transcendence is conceived. Barth never intended that his early stress upon God's utter transcendence of everything creaturely — a stress required in the then-current theological climate — should be taken as an *a priori* dogma. And it was to counter such a misapprehension that he later produced the counterstatements contained in *The Humanity of God,* in which he made clear that Christians cannot be content with a view of God stopping short with the concept of a "wholly other" (p. 45). And, because of Bultmann's "existential" view that we can speak of man without first "very concretely" having spoken of the living God (*ibid.,* pp. 56-57), he was prepared to leave behind his own alignment with Kierkegaard. Kierkegaard, indeed, had made it clear that for him time and eternity *were* brought together in the incarnation. Bultmann, however, developed his theology of demythologization precisely on the basis of the final unknowability of God. The issue at stake has been pinpointed by James D. Smart in *The Divided Mind of Modern Theology: Karl Barth and Rudolf Bultmann, 1908-1933.* Smart writes: "Crucial for Barth was the incarnation, that God became man in Jesus Christ, that the word of God was manifest in human flesh, concealed indeed in the humanity of Jesus but also revealed in it, and revealed in it in such a way that witness to that revelation *remains* the medium of revelation through all time. For Bultmann this was an absurdity. The humanity of Jesus was irrelevant to the revelation of which he was the bearer except in the bare fact (the *dass*) of its existence. The revelation was in his words and in the words that the church preached in dependence upon him, but concealed in them by the conceptual forms in which it was expressed. . . . The church's faith is centered for Barth not just in a kerygma but on

Law and Spirit in Revelation

The Word of the biblical God to men, therefore, is misrepresented when it is reduced, as Bultmann wishes to reduce it, to a supratemporal "event" that comes about "through" human words. In that case, the event-laden human words become no more than symbolic representations of that which cannot enter history but merely appears there in order to disclose a spiritual dimension within human self-consciousness. We are back again with Heidegger's view of language speaking in man and making audible the silence of Being. We are asked to believe man's existence to be very different from creaturely existence in history before the presence of the Creator. Man's real nature is disclosed in his capacity for receiving the eternal in the form of language, so that his words become symbols of the imageless transcendent. He is shown to belong to the dimension of history only accidentally, being essentially one with the infinite Word that no finite words can represent.

The biblical witness, on the other hand, is to the divine Word that can sound directly, and not merely symbolically, in history. This truth is represented in Isaiah's description (Isa. 55:8-11) of how the divine Word, though utterly beyond the self-imaginings of men, speaks from heaven and becomes, like the rain and the snow, actually present and active on earth. God's Word can enter human words and cause them to convey truly what the Sender wishes them to say. This divine Word does not simply "near" the eternal element to man's consciousness. It accomplishes the divine purpose in history.

It is sometimes said that, since God has no vocal organs,

---

a person to whom the kerygma points, and not on a person who is dead but on a person who is alive and active in the life of the world through his word and Spirit. Christian faith is faith in Jesus Christ and in God through Him" (p. 191). Barth in his *Church Dogmatics* writes: "By the grace of God we shall truly know God with our views and concepts, and truly speak of God with our words. But we shall not be able to boast about it, as if it is our own success, and we have performed and done it. It is we who have known and spoken, but it will always be God and God alone who will have credit for the veracity of our thinking and speaking" (II/1, 213).

He cannot really speak. Therefore our human talk about God "speaking" is symbolic, or mythic speech. Yet this objection is beside the point. Only an extremely naive person imagines that the divine Word can be called "word" solely if it happens to be produced in exactly the same way as human vocables are. We might as sensibly ask, in connection with Jeremiah's statement that in the new covenant God will write His law in men's heart (Jer. 31:33), whether He is to use a stylus or a felt-tip pen. The point is that, unless the Word of God is revealed authoritatively in human words, God is not related actually to His world. If men cannot hear and obey the Word of their maker concretely within their historical situation, the Word floats above the earth. The eternal and the temporal must remain forever divided. In that case, human nature can be, in Heidegger's words, *"appropriated* to that from whence we are called"[7] — that is, the eternal God can call to the eternal in man — but men cannot know the message of God for them in their individual lives.

It must be admitted that "dictation" theories of revelation sometimes seem to assume that God communicates His Word through vocables, so that understanding the exact sense of an aggregate of propositions is to receive the Word of God. This is surely to bind the divine Word to the measure of human words; for it is to say that we already have the words that can state all that God can possibly want us to know. We simply need to learn from God which of the verbal statements we encounter are true and which are false; and we have the authority of God Himself for being able to state without reservation that every statement found in Holy Scripture is true. Therefore, since we already know in principle the difference between true and false statements, faith in God consists essentially in the believing reception of each and every scriptural statement as objectively true.

The verbal approach to the Bible takes with full seriousness the authority of the Word of God. It guards against the danger of our presuming to claim to know better than God "what the case is" that makes a proposition true. For example, it rightly points out that human assumptions

---

[7] *Discourse on Thinking,* p. 90. Italics in the text.

concerning the universality of conditions governing man's biological existence cannot be made the basis for denying that Jesus of Nazareth was born of a virgin and rose physically from the state of death. It seems less adequate, however, in recognizing the authority of the Word of God over the use to which words may be put and over the extent of their meaning. The fact that words are in the Bible, and appear to form assertive statements, does not mean that our reading of them necessarily must yield authoritative statements that we can proceed forthwith to identify with the Word of God.[8] Were this the case, then the Bible, rather than being that inspired record which is able "to make us wise unto salvation through faith which is in Christ Jesus" (II Tim. 3:15-16), would be the written law of God.

What can be stated wholly in propositional terms, that is, in words that are understood to convey objective truth, appears necessarily under the aspect of law. Thus the end-product of the investigations of the experimental sciences are specific statements known as laws. A dictionary definition of law is: "something set, placed, fixed, laid down." The category of law embraces, indeed, all authoritative propositions that can be precisely and unambiguously expressed in words. The meaning of any law is its *literal meaning*. We can see how intimate the connection is between law and literal signification from the common phrase "the letter of the law." Also, it is well known that, in the realm of jurisprudence, the utility of a law is judged

---

[8] This is to attribute to Scripture what H. M. Kuitert in his book *Do You Understand What You Read? On Understanding and Interpreting the Bible* calls an "empty authority." Kuitert writes: "One cannot talk about the authority of Scripture unless he has his eye on the content of Scripture at the same time. And when we speak of the content of Scripture, we do not mean simply a great number of sentences that stand between Genesis 1:1 and Revelation 22:21. We have not even begun to speak of the content of the Bible when we have asserted that the Bible is God's Word from cover to cover. . . . To affirm the authority of the Bible apart from the Bible's own intention turns the authority of the Bible into an empty authority; and this kind of authority creates a situation in which the freedom of the children of God is traded for the tyranny of men" (p. 61).

to depend upon the certainty with which it can be interpreted. A law is no law if its meaning is doubtful.

Paul was referring directly to revelation as law when he made his often quoted (and often misinterpreted) reference to the letter that kills and the spirit that makes alive (II Cor. 3:6).[9] He was speaking of himself as a minister of the new covenant, a covenant not of the written word but of the Spirit. He began his discussion of the subject by speaking of his Christian brothers at Corinth as a living letter of words written by Christ upon their hearts. He continued by contrasting the new covenant foretold by Jeremiah with the giving of the covenant at Sinai. And his words have a very definite bearing upon the Christian understanding of the Bible.

If the final revelation of God is a revelation in terms of law, then certainly the authority of God's Word might well be wholly concentrated within a sacred book. This fact is substantiated in the history of Judaism. Although the Jewish community has never formulated any rigid theory of the inspiration of the Scriptures, yet the books of the Law have been vested with an authority that is, to all intents and purposes, final; while the Prophets and the Writings are regarded as having a lesser, dependent authority. But Paul was insistent on the new dimension of God's Word that has arrived with Christ and has set the revelation given to Israel in a new perspective. The Christian gospel is a proclamation of the new life

---

[9] From the time of the "Enthusiasts" of the sixteenth century to the present day this text has often been supposed to warrant the belief that the possession of the Spirit rendered superfluous any need for the text of Scripture. Behind all such assumptions lies the dogma of the eternal Word being voiceless, because transcending absolutely the phenomenal world. The truly spiritual man, therefore, has passed beyond any reliance upon words; since words belong to physical existence in space and time. It was in order to counter this type of thinking that T. S. Eliot once boldly reversed the Pauline words and asserted, "For the spirit killeth and the letter maketh alive." He did so in the context of his own concern for words as a poet and critic. But, at the same time, his "paradoxical" statement — which was most certainly not meant to contradict Paul — had a background in his Christian convictions concerning the centrality of the incarnation for understanding the relation between time and eternity, spirit and flesh.

WORDS AND THE WORD

in the Spirit; and Christians live in and by the witness of the Holy Spirit to the living Word.[10]

The gift of the Spirit, a gift announced by Jesus Christ at the end of His ministry and experienced by the church at Pentecost, is our reminder that the message which the living God graciously gives to men is nothing less than Himself. And therefore we receive the divine Word only when that Word is written on our hearts by the Holy Spirit. Nevertheless, we have to beware contrasting the spirit and letter of revelation in such an exclusive fashion that, in the effort to escape a mechanical literalism, we fall into an unscriptural spiritualism. In the same epistle in which he speaks of liberty given by the Spirit of the Lord, Paul warns the Corinthians against receiving "another spirit" than the Spirit they have received in Christ (II Cor. 11:4). If it is the Holy Spirit given by their Lord

---

[10] Antony Snell's book *Truth in Words* is largely concerned with exploring the authority of Scripture from such a perspective. Snell does not ask whether Scripture is authoritative for the Christian, for he assumes that it must be; but he asks how this authority manifests itself to the individual living within the community of the people of God that is the Christian church. He suggests (pp. 28-29) that we are mistaken if we first attempt to establish what texts are authoritative and then proceed to greet them "as definitive words of God," so that "our task is to assimilate and understand them, and then to use them as given premises for deduction whenever we are faced with intellectual or practical problems." Rather, he argues, authority for the Christian arises "from God having made us Christians," and so having called us to obey Him within the context of the life of the Church and the guidance of the Spirit. Thus the authority of texts "is not absolute, external, or prior." The authority of words is subordinate to the action of the living God upon His people called to take their place within the Body of Christ. While Snell writes out of a background of Anglo-Catholicism, in which Scripture has never been regarded as the sole rule of faith, but as sharing authority with Church tradition, his argument is capable of being expressed in terms appropriate to the Reformation principle of *sola Scriptura*. Writing from a Reformed position, H. M. Kuitert asserts that the purpose of reading Scripture must be primarily so that we can proclaim Christ. "To understand the intention of the Scriptures is nothing other than to understand the story of Jesus Christ in all its wide significance for our life and for the lives of all men." And the fact that the intention of the Scriptures has been fulfilled through the historical life of the Church is "the miracle of the Scriptures, the miracle of the Spirit" (*Do You Understand What You Read?*, p. 87).

who enables Christians to know the living God and to cry, "Abba, Father" (Rom. 8:15), then they must know that the God they address as Father is the same God who spoke to Israel in the giving of the Law. The witness of the Spirit to our spirits cannot be a purely internal witness having no connection with the history of God's calling of Israel or with the historical figure of Jesus of Nazareth, Israel's promised Messiah. The coming of the Son of the living God had indeed closed the old era of the Law, together with the exclusive worship at Jerusalem that the Law prescribed, so that henceforth the true worshippers should worship the Father in spirit and in truth (John 4:23). Yet the dawning of the new age does not abolish the historical actuality that salvation is "of the Jews" (John 4:22). Worship in spirit and in truth includes the recognition that human words are inadequate, so that our prayers must be given by the Spirit a meaning that we cannot verbalize (Rom. 8:26-27). At the same time we know the Spirit of God from other spirits, because He enables the human verbal confession to be made, *Christ has come in the flesh* (I John 4:3).

Life in the Spirit does not preclude the use of propositional statements made in words. It is, in fact, most intimately joined to these.

This is why a so-called "spiritual" (or allegorical) interpretation of Scripture is always inadequate. Were we able to validate the presence of the Holy Spirit out of the resources of our own spirits — if a divine element in us were continuous with the divine Word — it would then be possible to "go beyond" the words of the Bible and to indicate authoritatively what they "really" mean. Interpretation on the basis of a spiritual pre-understanding would be assumed without question. The idealistic evaluation of the language of the Bible as mythic language would be justified. But, in fact, God's revelation is inseparable from particular events in history; and the particularity of history disappears when historical events are read purely in terms of mythic meaning — as "meaning-events."

Paul, while contrasting the old covenant with the new as a "veiled" understanding of God's self-revelation awaiting a time of liberation by the Spirit, affirms, "Now the

Lord is that Spirit: and where the Spirit of the Lord is,
there is liberty" (II Cor. 3:17). But Paul's Lord was not
simply a "meaning-event," a Christ-idea uncovered by
Paul's faith. He was a historical person, Jesus of Nazareth,
the Word made flesh. The relationship between human
words and the divine Word can be properly found only in
Him.

The Word Who Is Person

"Accidental truths of history can never constitute the
proof of necessary truth of reason." Thus Lessing stated
the problem that has vexed thinkers after him for two
hundred years. Today Heinrich Ott finds Lessing's problem his own, though he would translate it into the form:
"Judgments of historical probability can never provide
the ground for the certainty of faith."[11] Ott's hope is to
solve the problem with help from Heidegger's theory of
language.[12] But, as we have seen, this is to dissolve historical existence into idealistic terms; and Ott's appeal to
"the ontological structure of human existence" discovered
in language is self-defeating. It is noteworthy that Ott
substitutes the phrase "the certainty of faith" for Lessing's
"necessary truth of reason." What Ott is seeking, evidently,
is a *spiritual* criterion for faith that is able to bypass
faith founded upon propositions relating to historical happenings. He wishes to find a gospel of the Spirit free from
the letter, a gospel of *meaning* without any dependence
upon *statement*, although he recognizes that Christians
are bound to a historically derived text.

All such wishes are bound to founder upon the stubborn
fact of historic Christian faith, which is faith in the Word
made flesh, the Word who Himself made statements in
human words and authorized the preaching of the gospel
concerning Himself in similar statements. If judgments of
historical probability can never provide the ground for the
certainty of faith, then that kind of certainty cannot be
the ground for faith in Jesus Christ. The hope to find an
escape from the conditions of historical existence is an illusion that is shattered upon the rock, the lordship of Christ,

---

11 "Language and Understanding," in *New Theology No. 4*, p. 130.
12 *Ibid.*, pp. 143-44.

which ensures our salvation in an altogether other manner.

So far I have pointed out a dilemma in our thinking about the certainty of faith. The authority of faith for us is bound up with the authority of the Bible in its propositional content. We cannot believe in the God of whom the Bible speaks by saying that the divine Word is found there spiritually but not essentially in just those words. If we say this, we elevate our internal spiritual consciousness above the scriptural statements, claiming that it is the divine element in us that validates the testimony of the Holy Spirit. On the other hand, if the Word speaks in words, do we need the Holy Spirit at all, since our human understanding (that comprehends words) furnishes us with the necessary means of understanding the Word?

John Calvin's *Institutes* seems to suggest the solution that the testimony of the Holy Spirit is required to allow us to submit our wills to recognize the authority of the words of the Bible (I.vii.1, 5). Calvin's argument was sound in its historical context, which was one of a war on two fronts (against the Roman Catholic subordination of the authority of the Bible to the authority of the Church, and against the Left Wing Reformers' trust in the "Inner Light" in place of the Bible). Yet, again historically, it has proved insufficient to prevent a lapse into legalism among those followers of Calvin who had gone beyond Calvin's robustly practical grasp of Christian faith to erect, as he did not, theories of verbally inerrant biblical inspiration.

Calvin was certainly justified in rejecting those who took Paul's words about the letter and the spirit as a charter for liberty to play fast and loose with Scripture. It is not so certain that he fully safeguarded the apostle's stress on the freedom from the Law that was won by Christ's coming. The Lord who makes all things new must surely have brought a new dimension to the human reception of the divine Word. Christians are not only those who add the New Testament to the Old, and who see now, in the Jewish scriptures, testimony to the coming Messiah. They must also be those who understand the divine Word in a new way, because that Word has come among them.

81

The new Christian understanding of the Word, and so of Scripture, is born of the fact that the Word of God — the same Word that spoke in the Law — was made flesh. He did not merely teach, telling us truths about God and ourselves in human word; He *was* the Word. He did not merely give us truths; He said, "I *am* the Truth" (John 14:6). Calvin himself, I believe, guides us toward a right understanding of the newness of the revelation that comes in Christ when he says that we have "no enjoyment of Christ, unless by embracing him as clothed with his own promises" (*Inst.* II.ix.3). These promises were, he points out, the same promises made in times of old. But he adds that "there is this difference to be observed in the nature or quality of the promises, that the Gospel points with the finger to what the Law shadowed under types" (*ibid.*).

The Word made flesh, then, is not to be known apart from the revealed Word of God in all the Scriptures. But He does put all Scriptures under His authority. He is the judge of Scripture, in the sense that He, and not we, says what Scripture *means*. He spoke with authority, and not as the scribes and lawyers, because He was the fulfiller of the Law. The scribes interpreted the Law from the standpoint of experts in human words, attempting to point out what the Law said *literally*. Jesus did not hesitate, on occasion, to interpret the Law in a sense seemingly quite opposed to its literal sense; yet not to destroy the Law, but to allow it to stand forth as the authentic revelation of the Father. In so doing, He showed that the divine Word could not be fully known apart from Himself and the promises He brought in His own person.

I should like to quote here a section from T. F. Torrance's *Theological Science,* a work that has greatly helped me personally to clarify my thoughts about faith and language. Torrance says that we see Christ "clothed with his promises" when we see Him as Word and Person united, that is, bringing together what normally we only know separately — since human words are, in our experience, always separable from the persons who speak them. Torrance writes:

This identity of Word and Person, then, is a primary characteristic of the Truth of God as it is in Jesus. It belongs to the nature of this Truth to be at once Person and Message, to be personal Being and yet communicable Truth. If it were only a communicated truth we would be thrown back upon ourselves to interpret Him. But because He is Person and Message in One, He is the Truth who both authenticates and interprets Himself. He is the Truth truthfully communicating Himself, and enabling us truthfully to receive Him. He is the Truth communicating Himself in and through truths, who does not communicate Himself apart from truths, and who does not communicate truths apart from Himself. It is a communication of truths, but of truths that cohere in the one unique Person of the Incarnate Word of God, and it is a personal encounter in life and being with Christ, but not in abstraction from a Message. It is personal Truth that not only comes to us in the form of Word, and therefore in and through Words, but has Word in its very content.

In other language, this is Truth that is both personal and propositional, but uniquely personal and uniquely propositional in the unique nature of Christ. ... Therefore our theological statements have a truthful reference to this Truth when that reference is at once personal and propositional, that is, dialogical.[13]

---

13 Pp. 147-48. Whenever the personal truth of God in Jesus Christ is removed from the center of Christian thinking in order to attempt a "nonobjectivizing" understanding of the divine Word, then the result is a general idea derived from human conceptualization. An example of this process can be seen in the basic argument of Dorothee Solle's *The Truth Is Concrete*. The title of the book derives from the Hegelian dictum that has been taken up by Marxism. Dorothee Solle claims that Christ's words to Pilate (John 18:36) set against Pilate's skepticism "his own particular truth, love" (p. 7). Similarly, Solle says — refusing to acknowledge that the words of Jesus Christ are authoritative from being the words of the Word — that Christ's words were established by God because they were words of a love that survived death. The word of love, being "the pure word . . . tells us about God." "In the beginning was love. . . . In it was life and the life was the light of men" (p. 81). Thus an abstract idea, an "it," takes the place of the personal incarnate Word of the New Testament. Christ is not any longer, in such a view, the one Name of our salvation. He becomes an illustration

In Torrance's insistence that Jesus Christ is at one and the same time Person and Word we can find, I believe, an escape from the dilemma of choosing between a legalistic understanding of the Holy Scripture and a falsely spiritualistic understanding of Christ wishing to part Him from "judgments of historical probability" in order to arrive at "certainty of faith." It is this same bridge, also, that can close the gap between theological language, which tends to absolutize certain forms of words and freeze faith into certain historically conditioned propositions, and living faith, which is by no means identical with doctrinal orthodoxy.

The question remains, however, as to whether recognizing the divine Truth as both Person and Word, as message and encounter, has practical consequences both in our understanding of faith and in our reading of the Bible; or whether it may not be a merely *verbal* solution, and therefore actually says very little in terms of our actual life as Christian believers.

In my final lecture I hope to apply what Torrance has to say about the "dialogical" nature of theological statements to the interpretation of the language of Scripture.

---

of Hegel's abstract definition of truth by virtue of his "pure" enunciation of a principle. The Word ceases to reveal God. Instead, we think *about* God in words which we happen to think suitable because they tell us what we would like to hear. A similar conclusion is reached by Fritz Buri in *How Can We Still Speak Responsibly About God?* Buri, like Jaspers, believes that words can serve merely as ciphers of transcendence, because God cannot be objectivized. He writes: "The task of theology is not to prove that God is love but to show how love constitutes the fulfillment of human existence (*Dasein*)" (p. 40). Again, it is assumed that human words constitute a final authority rendering unnecessary any divine Word. Theology is made into a way in which man speaks to himself about himself (or his self-conceived "world"). The rule of abstraction could hardly be extended further.

84

Chapter 4

Language and Scripture

AT THIS POINT THE OUTLINE OF A VIABLE HERME-
neutic has begun to appear. This hermeneutic will recognize the actualities of human language in our existence
and the authority of the divine Word as well. Thus it
aims at being both rational and believing.

It is necessary at this point to draw together the strands
of the previous lectures. I hope that some of the issues,
hitherto stated rather generally and abstractly, may stand
out more clearly as I illustrate them within the context of
the biblical record. Let me begin, then, by taking up again
the subject of myth as the matrix of language.

From what I said in the second lecture about the nature of myth as expressive language and about its limitation to the subjective mode of consciousness, you will gath-
er that I must deny that the message of the Bible is ever
given in the form of myth. The truth of Holy Scripture
cannot be identified with the subjective truth of myth.
Myth expresses the world as human subjects come to read
it in terms of their own relationship to it. But myth has
to be left behind as men learn that subjective meaning
and objective fact are not one and the same. If God is
objectively real, He must be decisively separated from
myth. If — being real — He gives us a revelation of Himself, then that revelation must have a propositional aspect
to it. It must tell us something about Himself, and about
our actual existence, and about the relation between the

two; something we could not know otherwise. It must give us information about what actually is.

For the whole Bible, the Lord — the earth's Creator and the earth's Redeemer — actually is. "He that cometh to God must believe that he is" (Heb. 11:6). This New Testament statement by no means stands alone, but follows through from the Old Testament's constant denunciation of idolatry. God *is*, therefore, in the way in which mythical deities *are not*. Certainly the gods of the nations supply a meaning for the lives of those peoples. If it were not so, there would be no need of warnings against idolatry as a temptation, and against the inroads of false worship upon the worship of the living God. The biblical protest is that idolaters are "vain in their imaginations" (Rom. 1:21) — they confuse actuality with a picture of the world that seems "meaningful" to them.

The language of Scripture, then, necessarily stands opposed to the language of myth. It places over against the subjective "meaning" of myth another criterion of meaning — objectivity.

Nevertheless, as we have seen, all language grows out of mythic thinking and still bears the marks of its origin. God has not, in fact, bypassed the human instrument of language in order to create another channel of communication altogether, one that might allow us to know objective truth directly and infallibly. Language is part of the world, and what Scripture says about the world in general can be applied to language too. Jesus prayed, not that His disciples should be taken out of the world, but that they should be kept from "the evil" (John 17:15). We might paraphrase these words, in order to apply them to the specific realm of biblical language, by saying that the Bible does not remove us out of the reach of mythic language, yet it allows us to avoid the untruth of myth.

Myth, Poetry, and the Bible

I have argued that language is made out of mythic patterns, but that mythic language develops into poetic language, where the subjective truths enshrined in primitive myths are no longer believed to describe objective reality directly, yet still mediate "meaning" to us. The truth of myth is that things can have no meaning for us until they are related to our subjective experience, until they are drawn into a meaningful imaginative pattern. The falsity of myth comes from projecting some imaginative pattern and thinking that this pattern must be the pattern of actuality, instead of being a merely possible pattern or imaginative exploration.

Kierkegaard acutely remarked that poetry is the art of the possible. Without poetic imagination nourished on the images of myth we would have no language with which to seek to distinguish truth from falsehood. But the poet, *qua* poet, does not concern himself with objective truth, but merely with subjective meaning. Certainly, no poet lives in a solipsistic universe, nourished on purely private images. He is always a most acute observer of the external world, and it is this that allows him to form new patterns of meaning. When the poet speaks of "the winter of our discontent," we understand better both the negativity of human feelings of dissatisfaction and the deadness of the winter season waiting to be transformed by the awakening life of springtime. Connecting the two, the poet brings new meaning to our experience. Yet he does not tell us anything about an objective connection between winter and discontent. If we think that we are discontented only because it is wintertime, or that throwing off discontent must end the winter season, we are back in the untruth of myth. In order for any such connection to make sense, we must leave poetry and turn to objective investigation. Conceivably, though, there *might* be such a connection. Poetry is the art of the possible. The opposite mode of thinking, scientific thought, itself relies upon the poetic imagination just as it relies upon language (although it tries as much as possible to escape from the subjectivities of language by using the sign-language of mathematics). Important breakthroughs in scientific investigation have come, again and again, through the poetic imagination. The "poetic" scientist imagines a possible connection between phenomena previously unrelated, and thus opens the way for investigation as to whether this possible connection is *actual*.[1]

---

[1] An interesting example of the "poetic" scientist is Sigmund

Poetry, as a literary form, precedes prose. This particular historical fact is not readily given credence by us today, because our cultural conditioning leads us to think of language as primarily a tool for gaining (or imparting) information. But, once we have grasped the mythopoetic roots of all language, we can overcome our bondage to the empirical vision. The modern assumption that there is a rigid division between poetry and prose is largely a conventional notion stemming from the custom of printing poetry so that it is instantly recognizable as *not* being prose. At the same time, there has grown the equally sharp categorization of poetry and prose fiction, on the one side, over against "history," "biography," and "factual reporting" on the other. Such distinctions reflect the growth of the empirical outlook and the valuations that have gone with it. Already in the sixteenth century Sir Philip Sidney wrote his *Apology for Poetry* because he felt it was needful "to make a pitiful defence of poor Poetry, which, from almost the highest estimation of learning, is fallen to be the laughingstock of children."

The Bible, of course, comes to us from a time before the modern categories of literary form arose. The Bible is full of poetry. And I argue that this is not accidental. It is because the Bible uses language to the full.

However, the Bible is not simply a book of "poems" — in the present-day sense. Far from being a series of exercises in the art of the possible, the Bible is concerned to communicate truth. Insofar as the Bible is the record of a dialogue between God and men, it is of course concerned with subjective truth; and therefore it employs poetic forms and symbolic language. I shall return to this point a little later. At present I wish to point out that, when the Bible does not bluntly denounce the falsity of myths that threaten belief in the actuality of the one

Freud. Freud was personally committed to an empirical outlook on the world — so much so that he records proudly how, when one of his children asked whether a story were true and was told that it was not, the child would turn away in disgust and take no further interest in the story (*The Future of an Illusion*, pp. 49-50). Yet he himself used classical myths to explain the workings of the psyche. Without his imaginative employment of these "untrue" stories his psychoanalytic theories could not have been developed.

true God, it neutralizes myth by giving to it only a poetic truth. In this way, it allows the pattern created by the myth to contribute to a better understanding of objective reality.

Scripture was composed in a milieu where myths were omnipresent. The language of Scripture, both in the Old and the New Testaments, gives ample evidence of that fact. The essential fact is, however, not that mythic patterns are everywhere evident in the Bible — its language would have been incomprehensible otherwise — but the way in which those patterns are employed. Whether we look at the elements of Sumerian, Babylonian, Phoenician, and Egyptian myths taken up into the biblical accounts of creation, or whether we look at the elements of Gnostic myths present in the New Testament descriptions of Christ the man from heaven, the result is much the same. The biblical language employs the imagery of myth, while transforming its content. Creation myths in which the gods wrested apart earth and heaven out of the body of the monster of Chaos account for some of the phrasing of the biblical account of creation. Yet the myths reflect the human imagination, contemplating (most likely) how the fullness of summer is wrested out of the inert body of winter, and then reading the process as an explanation "of the beginnings." The opening verses of Genesis, quite otherwise, tell essentially of the sole power of the one God who creates all things by His Word.

Similarly, consider the Gnostic spiritual man who deludes the archons and descends into the prison of the world in order to rescue the spirits there entrapped. This personage is a mythic presentation of man's experience of his being able to transcend time and space in thought, and of his feelings that, possessing such a power, he is inwardly divine and only externally bound to existence. The myth reappears as often as the human imagination contemplates its own inner powers. It lives again in our day in Heidegger's description of how man is *thrown* into existence and finds himself through opening himself to the quest for Being. But the New Testament description of the Word that comes down from God to be men's Savior by sharing their existence is one owing nothing to

89

the myth except some of the mythic imagery. The biblical message tells us, not about our eternal spiritual kinship with the heavenly man, but about the one actual individual, the man Jesus of Nazareth, who alone is God with us. Mythic imagery provided words by means of which first-century men might talk to their contemporaries. But the truth of Christ is known alone when men (then or now) acknowledge the actuality of His preexistence, life, death and resurrection. Myth knows many dying and rising gods — again, no doubt, deriving from human reaction to the winter-spring cycle. Yet the real question concerning Jesus the Savior is not of poetic possibility but of objective fact, "the events that have happened among us" (Luke 1:1, NEB). Lacking the mythic pattern that originally produced the necessary terminology, we should not be able to speak of Christ's death and resurrection. But all previous patterns of words must be strained to accommodate the revealed truth, namely, that *this man Jesus, the Christ of God* — no mere god among other gods, and no mere heavenly visitor of purely spiritual substance — suffered under Pontius Pilate and rose again. It is hardly surprising that Christian theology gave birth to a new terminology, one based on, yet breaking through, the language of Hellenistic philosophy.

Literal Truth and Literary Forms

In my first lecture I pointed out how empirical thinking always finds language to be a barrier between man and objective reality. For this reason, empirical thinkers do their best to do without language, with all its figurative and symbolic character deriving from its foundation in myth.[2] Language is necessarily ambiguous because it is born out of our subjective experience, which is always changing; and so they try to replace it with an artificial denotative sign-language — Hobbes' "counters" — that will unambiguously tell us "what the case is" in every event. While this desired freedom from language is finally im-

---

[2] This is, specifically, Russell's intention in recasting statements in order to expose their true logical form. In the last resort, Russell believes that a statement can be accurately formulated solely in the symbolic language of *Principia Mathematica*.

possible, scientific method has been able to reduce the subjective element in the language it uses to a minimum, largely through describing its subject-matter through the formal language of mathematics.

The aspects of experience that can be described clearly and unambiguously, however, are very limited. We have seen how the attempt to read objective reality in terms of the scientifically verifiable results in excluding from the realm of the real, not only God, but also nearly everything that has human meaning. This fact is properly relevant to theology, and to biblical hermeneutics in particular.

Revelation, I have argued, is not the truth of myth. Because it relates to the actual world and brings us actual information, it must be propositional. It describes "the events that have happened among us."

Yet, because revelation is given in human words, it cannot be more precise than language allows. The belief that the Bible consists of statements of *literal truth,* therefore, is ill-conceived. The notion of literal truth is quite correct if we oppose the *literal* to the *mythical* (or to the *allegorical,* to use an older terminology). In this sense we must say that God *literally* created the world, that He *literally* brought Israel out of Egypt, and that He *literally* raised Jesus from the dead. There is no way of explaining away the historical basis of our faith and also of submitting faithfully to the authority of the divine Word.

It is quite another matter, though, if we insist that all the statements of Scripture are literally true, and then proceed to interpret biblical statements in terms of modern ideas of factual accuracy. For this is to demand that language forged in other linguistic traditions shall conform to the pattern of language-usages familiar to us today; that is, to the usages developed since the sixteenth century, when empirical thinking began to assert itself over against the thought-forms of the prescientific consciousness — the period in which prose began to be rigidly separated from poetry. Instead of respecting historical actuality, this is to disregard it. It is to fail to take the patterns of biblical language with sufficient seriousness.[3]

---

[3] " 'Literal' is not synonymous with 'historical.' Inspiration does not imply that what is inspired must be understood literally, and

This particular defect is obvious enough when it results in riding roughshod over specific linguistic idioms; for example, when the biblical "forty days" is interpreted to mean that precise number of twenty-four-hour periods instead of a longish period of time rather than a shortish one. The grammatical structure of Hebrew alone is enough to show us that the Jewish people (even when writing in Greek) did not reckon time as we do today. (It is instructive to note, in this connection, that the attempt to establish the exact age of the earth from biblical data became a matter of importance only within the modern period; before then, no one thought of drawing that sort of information *literally* out of the scriptural record.)[4]

However, the principle of reading the Bible historically goes far beyond details of idiom to the whole structure of language-usage. To take one pertinent example, there is the question of the authorship of the biblical books. For a long time now, every author has been considered to have a proprietary right over his works. But the biblical books came out of a milieu in which such a concept was unknown, and where there was no issue of truth or falsehood involved in using a revered name in connection with writings by other hands. To assert literal authorship on the basis of contemporary ascription of authorship alone, therefore, is to apply an arbitrary standard of judgment. And the same principle applies — with exceedingly far-reaching results — when we take into consideration the former methods of editing texts, since these methods, while scrupulous about changing words, permitted large license in adding extra material and in transposing the order of the original.

Linguistic criticism, thus, runs without a break into historical criticism. But then, it may be asked, if the authority of the divine Word is made subject to canons adapted from the study of human words, what meaning

even less that everything must be viewed as having actually happened. . . . To put it bluntly, to accept everything reported in the Bible as having actually happened, one must tamper with the text"; H. M. Kuitert, *Do You Understand What You Read?*, pp. 59-60.

[4] For example, the biblical chronology of the King James Version is based upon the *Annals of the Old and New Testament* of Archbishop Ussher (1581-1656).

can this authority still bear? What sense is there of speaking about propositional revelation when each and every statement made in Scripture is subject to critical dissolution? Does this not turn Holy Scripture into just another human literary production? If we take upon ourselves to judge what is human and what is divinely inspired in Scripture, is this not subjectivism run mad?

Here the answer to such objections can only be that we are not reading the Bible *literally* — in the sense of reading what the words actually say — unless we read with a historical perspective; that the tools of scholarship, although always imperfect as anything human must be, are not used in order to judge the divine Word, but to understand it; and, indeed, that these tools are no more than an extension of the human ability to read and comprehend what is read, which is the indispensable condition of approaching the Scriptures at all. The end pursued remains forever the same, namely, the believing reception of the divine Word.

The excesses of the critical approach to Scripture come, not through recognizing that its words are human words, but through prejudging what it is that God reveals to us there. Literary and historical criticism errs seriously only when it claims to know with certainty absolute principles binding upon the intellect and therefore upon God's truth; when it tries to circumscribe the objective reality of His message to mankind.[5]

For example, it is sometimes urged that if we question the literal truth of part of the biblical record, we undermine the whole. If we say that the Book of Jonah is non-historical, we shall end by denying the resurrection of Christ. For the resurrection is something much more contrary to normal experience than anything described in the story of Jonah, and Christ Himself appealed to that story

---

[5] H. M. Kuitert wisely observes that not only is the Bible "time-bound" (in the sense of using the language and thought-forms proper to its historical origins) but all interpretation also is strictly time-bound (*Do You Understand What You Read?*, pp. 37-39). The limitations of those who interpreted Scripture in former ages is frequently very obvious to us. We ought to be well aware of the provisional nature of the conclusions contemporary critics reach, however "self-evident" these may appear to us.

in foretelling His rising again (Matt. 12:34-41). However, criticism does not question the historicity of Jonah on account of the miraculous elements in the story, but because of the literary form of the narrative. Although this narrative is traditionally included among the prophetic writings, it bears clear marks of belonging to another literary *genre*. Christ's own reference, also, is to the story, not to its historicity or nonhistoricity. He certainly does not seek to prove His resurrection by it, but uses it as a way of explaining its significance, parallel to His other saying, "Destroy this temple . . ." (John 2:19). The usage here is one of "typology" — recognized by Calvin, for example, as the way in which the Old Testament prefigures the New.

We cannot, under any circumstances, play fast and loose with the scriptural record, deciding for ourselves what is believable and what unbelievable. We must always endeavor to read *what is written,* since "all scripture is given by inspiration of God" (II Tim. 3:16). Yet it is equally binding the Bible to our human expectations to require that every part of the Bible have the same historical accuracy. Does God speak His Word to us only through history of the sort that we expect in a modern historical textbook? God's Word does not lie. But sometimes we are more ready than we have any right to be to instruct Him in what He must do to speak the truth.[6]

I am reminded of a story told me by an old Scotsman. He was a friendly person and an expert in Scots literature. Finding his mailman to be an intelligent individual having decided views of a number of subjects, he offered to lend him books from his library. The mailman said he would read no novels, for they contained nothing but foolishness. "Sir Walter Scott wrote novels which provide some wholesome reading," said my friend. "Yes," was the reply, "— and all lies!"

As a good Presbyterian, that mailman must have known

[6] For references to the views of the early church fathers concerning the nonhistorical elements in the early chapters of Genesis see J. K. S. Reid, *The Authority of Scripture: A Study of the Reformation and Post-Reformation Understanding of the Bible,* p. 24. Reid also emphasizes the freedom with which the Reformers interpreted Scripture.

that Jesus told parables. He probably never reflected that, as a literary form, the parable is as indifferent to historical veracity as is the novel. And he certainly would have been most indignant had he been told that his overly narrow concept of truth might prevent him reading his Bible with a heart that should "abound yet more and more in knowledge and all judgment" to "approve things that are excellent" (Phil. 1:9-10).

Holy Scripture is not in competition with the writings of men, so that attention given to the latter detracts from our obedience to the former. Rather, the more we are familiar with other books, the more we will find to wonder at in the inexhaustible riches of the Book of books. As we realize how easy it is to miss the meaning of a human author's words by placing preconceptions between us and what he is saying to us, we come to tremble lest we turn wilfully away from the leading of the Holy Spirit who alone can interpret to our spirits the Word of life. The freedom of Scripture to interpret itself is all too readily denied by our premature conclusions concerning interpretations assumed by us to be beyond question.

Parable as a Key Biblical Category

The parables of Jesus provide an essential pointer to the way in which the Word of God is related to human words. We are assured that our Lord's use of the parable was not accidental — "without a parable spake he not unto them" (Matt. 13:34).

As its name suggests, the parable is a juxtaposition of two meanings within a single framework of words. The words cannot simply be taken literally, on one level alone. When we grasp the literal meaning, we are aware that we have understood only in part. Thus the parable calls out for interpretation. And perhaps we may ask: Why is this roundabout method of communication necessary? Why are we not given the speaker's meaning directly and *in so many words*.

The Gospels record that the disciples asked Jesus this, and that the answer came with its echo of Isaiah's words about how the people close their ears to the Word of God (Matt. 13:11-17). Jesus reassured the disciples that they would have ears to hear. Yet even when their Master interpreted a parable to them, the disciples were taken back again to the human aspects of the parable by reference to which the divine message was given. The two aspects of the parable were inseparable.

From the aspect of literary form, a parable is a narrative that has left myth behind, having shed myth's claim to represent objective reality. Parable appears openly as a poetic creation. Because of this, it no longer appears as a story of the gods, but takes the form of an ordinary human story. Myths are literally unbelievable, yet are proposed for belief — either just as they stand (for a primitive audience), or after being demythologized (for a sophisticated audience). Parables are literally believable, yet they are offered as patent fictions. In short, parables are told for their meaning, for the Word revealed by means of words; but the words of the parable are not simply pointers to another world; their actual as well as their symbolic meaning is essential. Thus an interpreted parable is very different from a demythologized myth. The latter uses words as symbols for what is strictly wordless — Jaspers' "imageless transcendence," Heidegger's "depth of the height." This is because the mythic approach to existence is that it has no meaning in itself but only insofar as it reflects transphenomenal reality. A parable, quite otherwise, assumes that the divine reality its human words open to us, though literally beyond our comprehension, can actually be revealed to us by means of human words. Thus many of the parables of Jesus begin, "The kingdom of heaven is like. . . ." Certainly, the comparison is no more than a comparison. The kingdom of heaven cannot be brought down to earth for our inspection; it remains always a mystery. Yet Jesus could say to His disciples (as those who were capable of understanding the interpretation of parables), "It is given unto you to know the mysteries of the kingdom of heaven" (Matt. 13:11).

Parables, then, show how human words are capable of receiving the divine Word. They also show how the divine Word is not simply *written* but also *personal*. To know the words is not necessarily to understand the meaning of the parable. The Holy Spirit alone, directing our minds, is able to make the work of interpretation effective. In John's Gospel, the characteristic nature of parables is described as belonging to all the words of Jesus. Time and again, the hearers of the incarnate Word are shown to misunderstand, in a crudely literalistic way, some statement of Jesus concerning Himself and His mission. This is because *they do not know who it is that is speaking.* They imagine Him to be talking to them of reentering the womb (John 3:4); or about an unbelievably thirst-quenching water (4:15); or of insanely wanting to give people His flesh to eat (6:52); or of having seen Abraham within His lifetime (8:57). They are wholly unaware of the heavenly dimension of His humanly uttered words, because they do not believe in Him. They are unable, consequently, to see that He speaks with the authority of the divine Word. They stop short with the man Jesus, failing to perceive how this man is the Son of the Father; and how His words are the words of eternal life addressed personally to those who understand that the Scriptures testify to Him (John 5:39).

Parables, while carrying the subjective meaning of mythic language, declare the death of myth and the possibility of the divine Word speaking in human words. The whole of the New Testament (as John's Gospel dramatically illustrates) witnesses to the same truth. The gospel is no symbolical pointer to an utterly transcendent reality lying forever beyond human comprehension yet latent in the "depths" of the human spirit. Instead of directing us to pass beyond the "Jesus of history" in order to become aware of "the Christ of faith," the gospel directs us precisely to the Jesus of history who is the Christ which faith acknowledges in humble gratitude. The so-called Jesus of history — that good man and outstanding teacher who inspires us to have the same faith in God that He had — is a construction of the mythic imagination. He is the mirror image of the so-called Christ of faith, who is just another human being until our spiritual discernment discovers that His historically unimportant life is the locus of the Christ-event — the eternal shining through the temporal until it is reflected on our spiritual sensitivities. In this connection, one can see how Bultmann's historical skepticism concerning our knowledge of the life of Jesus is not simply the result of his reading of the New Testament documents. It is dictated in advance by his philosophical assumptions concerning the nonobjectivity of God.

Myth is the language of idolatry, the speech of those who have become "vain in their imaginations" (Rom. 1:21). It is idolatry to follow a Jesus of history, namely, one who is not God but reveals to us the divine quality immanent in our own thoughts and actions. It is idolatry to find the meaning of faith in a Christ-event, namely, the breaking into time of an eternal power that reveals to us the power of the divine immanent in our own self-consciousness. In either case the incarnate Word becomes transformed into a symbol of an unknown and unknowable God. His life, death, and resurrection are read as elements of a meaningful myth; while His words become echoes in human consciousness of oneness with the divine.[7]

The New Testament shows the human life of Jesus Christ, Word of the living God, in terms of a parable and not of a myth.

I previously defined parable as that mode of poetic language which has left myth behind. And I said that parables look at the actual world realistically, but not literally. Because poetry is the art of the possible, poetic or fictional parables are not actually real, though they are *lifelike*. The New Testament, however, does not present the story of Jesus as an imaginative poem but as complete

---

[7] An example of this approach is to be found in Owen Barfield's book *Saving the Appearances: A Study in Idolatry*. Speaking of Jesus Christ as "the Representative of Humanity," Barfield writes of the "I am" sayings in John's Gospel: ". . . and we shall reflect how near was the Aramaic dialect he spoke to Hebrew — so that at each 'I am' the disciples must almost have heard the Divine Name itself, man's Creator, speaking through the throat of man; till they can hardly have known whether he spoke to them or in them, whether it was his voice which they heard or their own" (p. 182). Here the view is that the historical event, namely, that the man Jesus Christ was actually speaking, is considered non-essential. What is essential is that the *idea* of divine-humanity was present in human consciousness; and therefore the historical and actual difference between Jesus and His hearers is simply passed over as unimportant. The timeless Word has found its locus within humanity wherever that Word reverberates in man's spirit.

actuality. ("If Christ be not raised, your faith is vain"; I Cor. 15:17.) Can there be historical parables?

There are certainly historical myths. The whole point of myth being subjective meaning, all that is required to make a myth is a mythic pattern. Such a pattern may be formed around any "named" thing whatsoever, whether real or fictional.[8] So, if I say to you, "That man is a regular Simon Legree," or "That man is a modern Nero," you will get my meaning. It matters not in the slightest that one is a fictional character and the other a historical person. Both names have come to symbolize inhumanity of a particular type. The so-called Christ-figures in modern literature are similar symbols. Even were Bultmann correct, and we knew nothing about the historical person of Jesus of Nazareth, Christ-figures would be just as effective poetically. For they represent the subjective understanding by authors of the "meaning" of the story of Jesus. They are reflection of myths explaining the Christ-event.

Parables, however, take the actual world seriously — even when they are poetic fictions. The patterns they weave have more than a subjective reference. We hear

---

[8] In *The Recovery of Christian Myth* Guilford Dudley III draws upon literature to reinforce his argument that Christianity today must recover the perspective of myth to repossess its authentic vitality and to avoid being overcome by the hidden myths of modernity. He uses the Book of Revelation to illustrate his argument. Insofar as Dudley is arguing for the recognition that "mythic patterns" underlie all our speaking, and asks the Christian to recognize the full range of these patterns that underlie the language of the Bible, he is surely right. He has very pertinent things to say about the way in which a mistaken compulsion to make Christian faith "reasonable" in order to meet the views of modern man has misled the churches into futile apologetic efforts, where some knowledge of modern literature would quickly show that ancient myth-patterns still move men's minds most powerfully. However, he fails to draw the distinction (partly because he accepts Jung's theory of myth too much) between "images" and "myth." That apocalyptic images are powerful and can be understood by modern man as fully as ever is something well worth saying today. The question still remains as to whether the language of the Apocalypse — and of the Bible as a whole — is to be considered as having an effect on our psyche similar to that of any other piece of literature, or whether it is to be regarded as conveying important and saving truth also. And the question of truth in relation to faith cannot be settled on the basis of myth.

the story told, and we say, "Yes, that's the way it is in life." The parables of Jesus *might* have been records of actual incidents, they are so realistic. An historical parable, therefore, cannot leave the hearer indifferent to the actuality of its human story. And, equally, it parts company from myth in the way it communicates an eternal message by means of its temporal narrative. The eternity of myth is subjective. We are caught up imaginatively into an eternal sacred time giving meaning to the flux of our lives. Yet that eternity may well be *only* subjective — in biblical terminology, it may be a "vain imagination." But, if an historical parable is to be true, it must be true on both the temporal and the eternal levels. It must have both subjective and objective actuality. It is because Jesus actually died and rose again that faith finds in these events the power of the living God made manifest. No one has ever seen God, and no human evidence can validate His power. Yet, having known the man Jesus and having been witnesses of His resurrection, the early church could interpret Him as the personal, historical Parable of the saving power of the Father. He was no mere symbol of that power. He was both son of man and Son of God, the Word of life that had been seen, heard, and handled (I John 1:1). As Paul said, Christ was no longer known "after the flesh" — simply as a human being (II Cor. 5:16); and therefore all humanity was now seen in the same light. Jesus actually died and rose again, so henceforth Christians were "dead" and their "lives hid with Christ in God" (Col. 3:3) — not literally, but not merely symbolically, either. By the Father's power those who have believed in the Son are *really* raised to eternal life in time and for eternity.

I am not arguing, of course, for parable to be regarded as the sole and exclusive form of language used in Scripture. The Bible exhibits within itself a great variety of literary genres displayed in books ranging all the way from national chronicles to apocalyptic visions and collections of hymns and aphorisms. What I am contending for is the view that, if we are to look for a "key" mode of language-usage in Scripture, then parable fits this position much more suitably than myth does.

The ahistorical nature of myth inevitably means that the possibility of a truth of revelation given in history is excluded. For this reason Karl Barth, more than twenty years ago (at a time when the application of mythic interpretation to the Bible was beginning to attract attention), objected to the absurdity of speaking of "creation myths." Creation was precisely something that myth can never encompass, so Barth insisted, because myths arise out of the attempt to explain the nature of the world as it unfolds before our consciousness.[9] Thus he argued that, supposing we need to apply some category to the early chapters of Genesis, the category of *saga* may best serve to preserve their historical dimension.

Saga suggests that the narratives in question were not conceived in terms of the literal description of empirical events that today we call "history." Their character is imaginative or "poetic," linking fact and legend in order to explain the significance of the past. Yet they are not mythic, either, although mythic elements may be embedded in them, for the purpose informing their telling is not to establish those timeless truths which are the concern of myths. The Bible is never interested in "meaning" divorced from the concrete existence of the people of Israel and God's revelation of Himself in their story.[10] History

---

[9] Barth writes: "At best a myth may be a parallel to exact science; that is, a myth has to do with viewing what has always existed and will exist. A myth has to do with the mighty problem that at all times propounds itself to man and therefore is timeless, the problem of life and death, of sleep and wakening, of birth and dying, of morning and evening, of day and night, and so on. These are the themes of myth. Myth considers the world as it were from its frontier, but always the world which already exists" (*Dogmatics in Outline*, p. 51). Barth's words about myth looking at the world "from its frontier" are confirmed by Eliade's characterization of myth as dealing essentially with man's condition "at the beginnings." The "primal events" of myth, so Eliade explains, illumine the present situation of humanity in terms of happenings *in illo tempore* — "once upon a time." Here again, we see how for mythic thinking "world" and "self" are really synonymous.

[10] So Barth writes: "The Bible speaks in Genesis 1 and 2 of events which lie outside historical knowledge. But it speaks upon the basis of knowledge, which is related to history. In fact, the wonderful thing about the biblical creation narratives is that they stand in strict connection with the history of Israel and so with the

and prehistory alike are set explicitly in the context of Israel's relation with the living God who is outside history as well as active within it. Consequently, the telling of Israel's history involves the parabolic mode. There is continuity in the "moral" meaning of the story of Adam's expulsion from the garden (Gen. 3:17-24), of Isaiah's "Song of the Vineyard" (Isa. 5), and of Christ's Parable of the Vineyard (Mark 12:1-12). All three tell of God's care for His people, and the people's faithlessness.

It follows that all attempts to find in myth the key category of Christian faith end by de-historicizing this faith, turning it into a wholly general message about the resources contained in humanity as such for establishing itself and for developing its "spiritual potential" in a "meaningful" manner.[11] But that is to make faith an idea latent in our self-consciousness, a self-understanding disclosing to us a "world" that is meaningful to us because it affirms the findings of our own inner vision. In making our choice of "faith" on the basis of a mythic reading of the gospel message, we simply assimilate it to some prior view we have adopted about the total meaning of life.[12]

story of God's action in the covenant with man. According to the Old Testament narrative, this begins with God's having created heaven and earth. The first and second creation accounts alike stand plainly in connection with the theme of the Old Testament: the first account shows the covenant in the institution of the Sabbath as the *goal*, the second account as the *continuation* of the work of Creation" (*ibid.*, pp. 51-52).

[11] Thus Charles J. Ping in *Meaningful Nonsense* avers about myths that "their permanent value lies in the power to present significant life orientations" (p. 113). *Myth and Ritual in Christianity* by Alan Watts is a consistent presentation of the mythic patterns of Christianity as a *philosophia perennis* divorced from historical actuality. Brevard S. Childs' *Myth and Reality in the Old Testament,* in contrast, shows how radically the biblical writers transform all the mythic material they use.

[12] Reinhold Niebuhr assumes that Paul's words "as deceivers, and yet true" (II Cor. 6:8) can be understood in a "profound" fashion to illuminate how religious language is always symbolic language. In his sermon "As Deceivers, Yet True" (in *Beyond Tragedy: Essays on the Christian Interpretation of History*), he writes: "Christ, who expresses both the infinite possibilities of love in human life and the infinite possibilities beyond human life, is thus a true revelation of the total situation in which human life stands" (p. 17). Niebuhr thus assumes that we already know, apart from revelation, what the

This can come about only when we do not really recognize history. From this viewpoint, history can be nothing more than the temporal and spatial scroll upon which transphenomenal meaning is written and unrolls to exhibit that meaning to our consciousness.

Indeed, exponents of faith-as-myth, for the most part, do not speak about history. If they are consistent, they prefer the word *historicity* — which is quite another thing. Bonhoeffer once remarked that the concept of personality is itself nonpersonal. Equally, the concept of historicity is nonhistorical. It does not expect anything new to appear out of the dimension of history, since all that can be said about the "world" is already assumed to have been laid down in advance, being in principle contained within the concept. Biblical faith, on the contrary, finds the focus of faith in the living God. The living God is precisely the one who cannot be bounded by any concept. His revelation cannot be known until He reveals it — in history. Unlike myth, parable is tied to the historical dimension. Parables draw their material from human existence in its concrete actuality. They then refer the *meaning* of that actuality to the living God who has created it and reveals His Word within it, without being encompassed by it or limited to it. Mythic thinking deals in Christ-events. The symbol "the Christ" is only one possible symbol out of many other possibilities, and thus a Christ-event is endlessly repeatable and has no essential dependence upon the man Jesus of Nazareth. Parabolic thinking knows "the Christ" solely as the One so designated by the living God. Only that One who Himself brings God's kingdom can tell parables of the kingdom.

Relating the Divine to the Human

My conclusion, then, is that biblical language should not be regarded as being *either* literal *or* symbolic. The words of Scripture are thereby not forced into an alien framework in which their message cannot be heard. Instead, the Bible speaks to us, in the Holy Spirit, with words

total situation of human life is. Christ is the concrete universal illustrating in time and space man's consciousness of the Absolute of love that moves in his own spirit.

which communicate both actuality and parabolic meaning. The incarnate Word Himself *is* this Word; a Word that comes to us, who see as yet "through a dim reflection in a mirror" (I Cor. 13:12 — Jerusalem Bible), in two modes — an earthly and a heavenly — but yet is one Word.

Theology, whose task it is to make explicit the implications of biblical language within the church for the needs of Christian confession of the full gospel of Jesus Christ, follows this twofold pattern.

For instance, there is the question of "salvation history." Clearly, the gospel cannot be explicated faithfully in terms of modern history, which assumes an empirical limit to the events which are to be taken as "historical." Neither God's active rule over history nor His participation within history by means of the incarnation can enter the secular historian's work, even should he happen to be himself a Christian believer. Therefore a framework for history which admits the causality of the living God has to be given; one allowing the historical events that faith confesses to be seen from the perspective of Christian faith. Salvation history has to be understood as the necessary explanation of the "sacred" events which themselves belong to history and can be recorded by modern historical methodology. Yet, to set up a strict division between transhistorical truth (*Geschichte*) and empirical history (*Historie*), as Bultmann does, is to reintroduce the mythic pattern and to create an impassable gulf between *event* and *meaning*, a gulf only verbally bridged by the notion of "historicity." History — in the sense of a record of human happenings — and salvation history — in the sense of human happenings seen in the light of God's self-revelation — can neither be assimilated to each other nor sealed off in watertight compartments.

Under no circumstances will the believer wish to bend the facts to fit his beliefs, to distort the record of *what actually happened* in order to make this fit the contours of his creed. Yet neither will he be willing to accommodate his creed to the empirical historian's *a priori* conclusions that the beliefs of the Christian community cannot possibly be true because "history" cannot admit the notion of God acting in history. The theologian must insist that, for those to whom the history of Israel is the record of God's saving purpose for mankind, *this history* is at once human history and saving history. Actual events find their meaning in God's purpose. Yet the events themselves are not simply the occasion of God's revelation, which then shines through the events; but the events are themselves material of the revelation. Just as a parable requires experience of actual life-situations in order for its message to be received, so salvation history can be received only when its historical basis in the human world is accepted as authentic and actual.

Again, to consider another theological theme, theology has never found a way of speaking of the one incarnate Lord except by positing a division within Him. He is spoken of as one person having two natures — the human and the divine. This way of speaking reflects the reality of the understanding of the incarnation as this reality impinges upon our lives as existing human beings. Christ is like us, a Man among men. He is also unlike us, very God of very God. Wherever an attempt has been made to overcome this formula in order to reach some unitary statement, the result has always been to lose hold of either the real humanity of Jesus Christ or else to make His divinity problematic and less than an actual revelation of the living God.

One way of attempting to escape the duality of the two-nature doctrine is to regard Christ as symbolizing the essence of humanity as infinite in spirit while finite in temporal manifestation. Christ then becomes the "concrete universal" typifying the unity of divine and human elements in the human spirit.[13] Recently, Wolfhart Pannen-

---

[13] In "As Deceivers, Yet True" Reinhold Niebuhr writes: "In Christian thought Christ is both the perfect man, 'the second Adam' who had restored the perfection of what man was and ought to be; and the Son of God, who transcends all possibilities of human life. It is this idea which theology sought to rationalize in the doctrines of the two natures of Christ. It cannot be rationalized and yet it is a true idea. Human life stands in infinity" (*Beyond Tragedy*, p. 16). In Niebuhr's thinking it is the "idea" that counts. Whether Christ, in fact, was God and man does not matter, and to say that He was is a "deception" — a deception that gives us a myth with which to make meaningful our human situation with its "openness" to the infinite and the eternal. Similarly, Nels Ferré draws from his reading

berg's book *Jesus — God and Man* tries to dispense with the two-nature doctrine in favor of the "concept" of the divine-human unity. The result is that Pannenberg concludes that "all statements of Christology have only metaphorical meaning." Since "only the eschaton will ultimately disclose what really happened in Jesus' resurrection from the dead,"[14] we can speak now simply of its significance in symbolic form. Hence Pannenberg has emptied the resurrection of all actuality, and has slipped back into a mythic form of interpreting the person of Jesus Christ. The incarnate Word is forbidden to speak to us really, and it is forced to give no more than symbolic utterance. Revelation is put into the future. The Father may yet speak — but He has not already spoken decisively in the Son.

We are back, then, with the issue which Athanasius faced so forthrightly in his dispute with Arius. T. F. Torrance, in his essay "The Problem of Theological Statement Today,"[15] has shown that Athanasius dealt precisely with those matters which are at the center of dispute today. In the struggle over the *homoousion*, the issue of language was raised and considered by Athanasius in great detail. If we are not justified in accepting from Scripture the full unity of the Son with the Father, so Athanasius argued, this assumes that the human words we speak are incapable of declaring the truth about God, except symbolically. The Arians assumed that God could never truly enter the temporal sphere. Jesus could not be the incarnate Word. Therefore scriptural language about Jesus is to be interpreted as a human way of speaking about the unknowable. The Arians, therefore, substitute mythic-speaking (*mythologein*) for speaking under the real revelation of God (*theologein*). Torrance indicates the importance for Athanasius of theological statements made *paradigmatically*, that is, in words embodying representations (*paradeigmata*) of human things in order to speak of realities beyond human experience. (This corresponds very

of the "Christ-event" the conclusion that human life stands in infinity. In *The Universal Word* he comments: "The historic Christ is the concrete universal which the historic Jesus enacted" (p. 169).

[14] P. 397.

[15] *Theology in Reconstruction*, pp. 46-61, especially p. 48.

closely to what I have called *parabolic* language.) God takes up our human language into His own truth. Because the eternal Word has come in the flesh, we can know that human words are not incapable of expressing divine reality. It is pagan to think that we can do no more than form picture-images of the incomprehensible divine reality. Scripture mediates to us the Word of God Himself, showing us God acting towards us in accordance with His own divine purpose.

One might continue through the whole range of theology, finding always the need to state both the way in which God's Word is spoken on earth and the heavenly origin of that Word. I shall conclude with a brief glance at the theology of prayer.

On its human side prayer is words uttered by men. But words do not by themselves constitute prayer. Empiricists would conclude that a praying man is actually speaking to himself; though perhaps in so doing he may be putting himself into the right frame of mind for constructive moral and social action.[16] Idealists would believe that all prayer is essentially wordless, and is most completely exemplified in contemplation; for there the individual soul is made aware of its grounding in the Divine Spirit. When Paul speaks of our inability to pray and of the Spirit who supports us in prayer with unutterable words (Rom. 8:26-28), this might be thought to support the idealistic view.[17] But, in fact, Paul is here directing us to the dual nature of Christian prayer, in which human words cannot by themselves constitute prayer but all true prayer is prayer "in the Spirit."

We can pray, just as we can hear God's Word in Scripture, only when the Spirit enables us. Prayer is made neither by our words or by our wordlessness. It is a gift of grace. Yet it is not apart from our praying that God gives His gift of prayer. Prayer is also that to which God calls us. We are commanded to pray, to address

---

[16] This is the conclusion of Paul van Buren in *The Secular Meaning of the Gospel,* pp. 188-190.

[17] Tillich quotes Paul's words here in support of his idealistic interpretation of prayer as best understood through the contemplative mode. See *Systematic Theology,* III, 192.

God after our human, earthly fashion; and to pray in faith, believing that God hears us and blesses our prayers.[18] Therefore prayer cannot be primarily a moral activity intended to improve us or hearten us. And it cannot be primarily an experience of spirituality, an entering into the "depth dimension" of existence. It is an act in which we are called to speak on earth, saying, "Our Father," so that the Word from heaven may be born in us. When we pray "in the name of Jesus," we encounter the Word that came in Jesus to earth for our salvation, the Word that is both human and divine.

Human and divine! The amazing gift of the Father who sent His Son into the world for the salvation of sinners is the unshakable foundation of our faith. It also is the only possible starting-point for a Christian theological understanding of language. I come now back to my starting-point. Language cannot simply be a humanly formed instrument for coming to know the physical world in which we are set — a tool that can be thrown away when it has served its purpose. Empiricism cannot give us the whole truth about language, although it can teach us that the purpose of language is to accept objective reality for what it is in itself, not simply as it appears to us to be. And language cannot be an ultimate reality-in-itself, a divine power emanating from infinite, imageless transcendence and manifesting itself symbolically in finite images. Idealism cannot give us the whole truth about language, although it can remind us that we are subjects who seek meaning in the world and cannot simply walk outside of ourselves to find objective truth apart from our experience as subjects.

Language is neither a tool at our disposal nor a divine voice that speaks within us, bringing us intimations of

---

[18] This is most pertinently and cogently set out in Jacques Ellul's book *Prayer and Modern Man.* Ellul shows that, because prayer is not ordinary speech, the "problem of language" cannot affect the theology of prayer. Our root problem, Ellul affirms, is our unwillingness to pray, to be *not faithless but believing,* and so our refusal to hear the voice of the living God who addresses us in grace. Prayer calls us to a relationship with the God of grace, and "is indeed a question of duty expressed in a summons" (p. 104), as well as a gift of the Spirit.

our own essential divinity. It is the gift of God to His creatures, whom He has made in His own image, able to enter into community with Him. It is a gift which, as with all His gifts, we have misused and perverted. He alone can restore to us His own gift, renewed through His gracious forgiveness of sinners. And that forgiveness comes through the gift of His Son. Through belief in Him, and through the power of His cross and resurrection, we may learn how to speak once more as children of our Father.

All language, the gift given by God, must return to Him in gratitude and thanksgiving. As scholars in the school of Christ, we may learn to speak under the direction of the Holy Spirit the loving language of the kingdom. The beginning of all true speaking is to learn that God's Word has indeed come to us to show us how words may be true. The first lesson of the kingdom is to be able to say, "Jesus Christ is Lord."

Works Cited and Suggestions for Further Reading

Alston, William P. *Philosophy of Language*. Englewood Cliffs, N. J.: Prentice-Hall, 1964.

Altizer, Thomas J. J., William A. Beardslee, and J. Harvey Young (eds.). *Truth, Myth, and Symbol*. Englewood Cliffs, N. J.: Prentice-Hall, 1962.

Auerbach, Erich. *Mimesis: The Representation of Reality in Western Literature*. Princeton, N. J.: Princeton U. P., 1953.

Austin, J. L. *How to Do Things with Words*. New York: Oxford, 1965.

———. *Sense and Sensibilia*, reconstructed from the manuscript notes by G. J. Warnock. New York: Oxford, 1962.

Ayer, A. J. *Language, Truth and Logic*. New York: Dover, 1936.

Barfield, Owen. *Saving the Appearances: A Study of Idolatry*. New York: Harcourt, n.d.

———. *Speaker's Meaning*. Middletown, Conn.: Wesleyan U. P., 1967.

Barth, Karl. *Church Dogmatics*, Volume II, "The Doctrine of God," First Half-Volume. Naperville, Ill.: Allenson, 1957.

———. *Dogmatics in Outline*. New York: Harper, 1949.

———. *The Humanity of God*. Richmond, Va.: John Knox, 1960.

Bartsch, Hans Werner (ed.). *Kerygma and Myth*, Volume II. Naperville, Ill.: Allenson, 1962.

Bendall, Kent, and Frederick Ferré (eds.). *Exploring the Logic of Faith*. New York: Association, 1962.

Bevan, Edwyn. *Holy Images: An Inquiry into Idolatry and Image-Worship in Ancient Paganism and in Christianity*. London: Allen & Unwin, 1940.

———. *Symbolism and Belief*. London: Allen & Unwin, 1938.

Bodkin, Maud. *Studies of Type-Images in Poetry, Religion, and Philosophy*. London: Oxford, 1951.

Bolle, Kees W. *The Freedom of Man in Myth*. Nashville: Vanderbilt U. P., 1968.

Braithwaite, R. B. *An Empiricist's View of the Nature of Religious Belief*. Cambridge: Cambridge U. P., 1955.

Brown, James. *Kierkegaard, Heidegger, Buber, and Barth: Subject and Object in Modern Theology*. New York: Collier, 1955.

Bultmann, Rudolf. *Faith and Understanding, I*. New York: Harper, 1969.

111

Buri, Fritz. *How Can We Still Speak Responsibly About God?* Philadelphia: Fortress, 1967.

Campbell, C. A. *On Selfhood and Godhood.* New York: Humanities, 1957.
Campbell, Joseph. *The Flight of the Wild Gander: Explorations in the Mythological Dimension.* New York: Viking, 1969.
Cassirer, Ernst. *Essay on Man.* Garden City, N. Y.: Doubleday, 1944.
———. *Language and Myth.* New York: Harper, 1946.
Childs, Brevard S. *Myth and Reality in the Old Testament.* Naperville, Ill.: Allenson, 1962.
Cornford, F. M. *From Religion to Philosophy: A Study in the Origins of Western Speculation.* New York: Harper, 1957.
Cullmann, Oscar. *Christ and Time: The Primitive Christian Conception of Time and History.* Philadelphia: Westminster, 1951.
———. *Salvation in History.* New York: Harper, 1967.
Cunliffe-Jones, H. *The Authority of the Biblical Revelation.* London: James Clarke, 1945.

Dillistone, F. W. *Christianity and Symbolism.* London: Collins, 1955.
Dudley, Guilford, III. *The Recovery of Christian Myth.* Philadelphia: Westminster, 1967.

Ebeling, Gerhard. *God and Word.* Philadelphia: Fortress, 1967.
———. *The Problem of Historicity.* Philadelphia: Fortress, 1963.
———. *Word and Faith.* Philadelphia: Fortress, 1963.
Eliade, Mircea. *Cosmos and History: The Myth of the Eternal Return.* New York: Harper, 1959.
———. *The Sacred and the Profane: The Nature of Religion.* New York: Harcourt, 1959.
———. *Myth and Reality.* New York: Harper, 1963.
———. *Patterns in Comparative Religion.* New York: Meridian, 1963.
Ellul, Jacques. *Prayer and Modern Man.* New York: Seabury, 1970.
Evans, Donald. *The Logic of Self-Involvement.* New York: Herder and Herder, 1963.

Fawcett, Thomas. *The Symbolic Language of Religion: An Introductory Study.* London: S.C.M., 1970.
Ferré, Frederick. *Language, Logic, and God.* New York: Harper, 1961.
Ferré, Nels F. S. *The Universal Word: A Theology for a Universal Faith.* Philadelphia: Westminster, 1969.
Flew, Antony, and Alasdair MacIntyre. *New Essays in Philosophical Theology.* New York: Macmillan, 1955.
Freud, Sigmund. *The Future of an Illusion.* Garden City, N. Y.: Doubleday, 1957.
Fuller, Reginald H. *The New Testament in Current Study.* New York: Scribner, 1962.
Funk, Robert W. (ed.). *Journal for Theology and the Church.* New York: Harper. Volume 1. James M. Robinson, *et al. The Bult-*

mann School of Biblical Interpretation: New Directions? (1965). Volume 2. Rudolf Bultmann, *et al. Translating Theology into the Modern Age* (1965). Volume 4. Wolfhart Pannenberg, *et al. History and Hermeneutic* (1967).

Gilkey, Langdon. *Naming the Whirlwind: The Renewal of God Language.* Indianapolis: Bobbs-Merrill, 1969.

Grant, Robert M. *A Short History of the Interpretation of the Bible,* revised edition. New York: Macmillan, 1963.

Harvey, Van Austin. *The Historian and the Believer.* New York: Macmillan, 1966.

Hegel, Friedrich. *On Christianity: Early Theological Writings.* New York: Harper, 1961.

Heidegger, Martin. *Discourse on Thinking.* New York: Harper, 1966.

Hick, John. *Faith and Knowledge.* Ithaca, N. Y.: Cornell U. P., 1957.

High, Dallas M. *Language, Persons and Belief: Studies in Wittgenstein's 'Philosophical Investigations' and Religious Uses of Language.* New York: Oxford, 1967.

——(ed.). *New Essays in Religious Language.* New York: Oxford, 1969.

Hodges, H. A. *Languages, Standpoints and Attitudes.* London: Oxford, 1953.

Hordern, William. *Speaking of God: The Nature and Purpose of Theological Language.* New York: Macmillan, 1964.

Jaeger, Werner. *Theology of the Early Greek Philosophers.* New York: Oxford, 1968.

Jaspers, Karl. *Myth and Christianity.* New York: Noonday, 1958.

Jenson, Robert W. *The Knowledge of Things Hoped For: The Sense of Theological Discourse.* New York: Oxford, 1969.

Kuitert, H. M. *Do You Understand What You Read? On Understanding and Interpreting the Bible.* Grand Rapids: Eerdmans, 1970.

Lefevre, Perry (ed.). *Philosophical Resources for Christian Thought.* Nashville: Abingdon, 1968.

McDonald, H. D. *Ideas of Revelation: An Historical Study, A.D. 1700 to A.D. 1860.* London: Macmillan, 1959.

Mackinnon, Donald M. *Borderlands of Theology and Other Essays.* New York: Cambridge, 1961.

MacQuarrie, John. *God-Talk: An Examination of the Language and Logic of Theology.* New York: Harper, 1967.

Marty, Martin E., and Dean G. Peerman (eds.). *New Theology No. 4.* New York: Macmillan, 1967.

Mascall, E. L. *Words and Images.* London: Longmans, Green, 1957.

Mitchell, Basil (ed.). *Faith and Logic: Oxford Essays in Philosophical Theology.* New York: Humanities, 1958.

113

Niebuhr, Reinhold. *Beyond Tragedy: Essays on the Christian Interpretation of History.* New York: Scribner, 1938.

Pannenberg, Wolfhart. *Jesus — God and Man.* Philadelphia: Westminster, 1968.
Paton, H. J. *The Modern Predicament.* London: Allen & Unwin, 1955.
Picard, Max. *Man and Language.* Chicago: Regnery, 1963.
Ping, Charles J. *Meaningful Nonsense.* Philadelphia: Westminster, 1966.
Pole, D. *The Later Philosophy of Wittgenstein.* New York: Oxford, 1958.
Preus, Robert. *The Inspiration of Scripture.* Edinburgh: Oliver & Boyd, 1955.

Ramm, Bernard. *Special Revelation and the Word of God.* Grand Rapids: Eerdmans, 1961.
———. *The Witness of the Spirit.* Grand Rapids: Eerdmans, 1960.
Ramsey, Ian T. *Christian Discourse: Some Logical Explorations.* New York: Oxford, 1963.
———. *Religious Language: An Empirical Placing of Theological Phrases.* New York: Macmillan, 1963.
Reid, J. K. S. *The Authority of Scripture: A Study of the Reformation and Post-Reformation Understanding of the Bible.* London: Methuen, 1957.
Robinson, H. Wheeler. *Inspiration and Revelation in the Old Testament.* Oxford: Clarendon Press, 1946.
Robinson, James, and John B. Cobb (eds.). *New Frontiers in Theology.* New York: Harper. Volume 1. *The Later Heidegger and Theology* (1963); Volume 2. *The New Hermeneutic* (1964); Volume 3. *Theology as History* (1967).
Rubenstein, Richard. *After Auschwitz: Radical Theology and Contemporary Judaism.* Indianapolis: Bobbs-Merrill, 1966.
Russell, Bertrand. *An Inquiry into Meaning and Truth.* New York: Humanities, 1940.
———. *The Principles of Mathematics.* New York: Norton, 1938.

Scheler, Max. *On the Eternal in Man.* New York: Harper, 1961.
Smart, James D. *The Divided Mind of Modern Theology: Karl Barth and Rudolf Bultmann, 1908-1933.* Philadelphia: Westminster, 1967.
Smethurst, Arthur F. *Modern Science and Christian Beliefs.* London: Nisbet, 1955.
Snell, Antony. *Truth in Words.* London: Faith Press, 1965.
Solle, Dorothee. *The Truth Is Concrete.* London: Burns & Oates, 1969.
Stevenson, W. Taylor. *History as Myth.* New York: Seabury, 1969.

Tavard, George H. *Holy Writ or Holy Church.* London: Burns & Oates, 1959.

114

Thornton, L. S. *Revelation and the Modern World*. Naperville, Ill.: Allenson, 1950.

Tillich, Paul. *Systematic Theology*, Volumes I, II, & III. Chicago: U. of Chicago, 1951, 1957, 1964.

Torrance, Thomas F. *Theological Science*. London: Oxford U. P., 1969.

———. *Theology in Reconstruction*. Grand Rapids: Eerdmans, 1965.

Urmson, J. O. *Philosophical Analysis*. New York: Oxford, 1956.

Van Buren, Paul. *The Secular Meaning of the Gospel: Based on an Analysis of Its Language*. New York: Macmillan, 1963.

Watts, Alan W. *Myth and Ritual in Christianity*. Boston: Beacon, 1968.

Wheelwright, Philip. *The Burning Fountain: A Study in the Language of Symbolism*, new and revised edition. Bloomington: Indiana U. P., 1968.

White, R. E. O. *Open Letter to Evangelicals: A Devotional and Homiletic Commentary on the First Epistle of John*. Grand Rapids: Eerdmans, 1964.

Wilson, John. *Language and the Pursuit of Truth*. New York: Cambridge U. P., 1967.

Wittgenstein, Ludwig. *Lectures and Conversations on Aesthetics, Psychology and Religious Belief,* compiled from Notes taken by Yorick Smythies, Rush Rhees and James Taylor, edited by Cyril Barrett. Berkeley: U. of California, 1967.

———. *Philosophical Investigations*. New York: Barnes and Noble, 1953.

———. *Tractatus Logico-Philosophicus*. New York: Humanities, 1961.

Zahrnt, Heinz. *The Question of God: Protestant Theology in the Twentieth Century*. New York: Harcourt, 1969.

Zuurdeeg, Willem F. *An Analytical Philosophy of Religion*. Nashville: Abingdon, 1958.

Index of Names and Subjects